Robert Burns – The Freemason

Robert Burns – The Freemason

Edited by
JOHN WEIR
DSO, OBE, JP, MA, FEIS

First published in the United Kingdom 1996

© 1996
The Grand Lodge of Scotland

Edited by Brother John Weir and published by Ian Allan Regalia Ltd, Coombelands House, Coombelands Lane, Addlestone, Surrey KT15 1HY, under the authority of The Grand Lodge of Scotland, by Grand Secretary, Freemasons' Hall, 96 George Street, Edinburgh EH2 3DH.

Printed by IAN ALLAN PRINTING Ltd
Coombelands House, Coombelands Lane, Addlestone, Surrey KT15 1HY

ISBN 0 85318 213 2

British Library Cataloguing in Publication Data.
A catalogue record for this book is available from the British Library

CONTENTS

LIST OF ILLUSTRATIONS

ACKNOWLEDGMENTS

I should like to express my thanks to the Grand Secretary of the Grand Lodge of Scotland, the Curator of the Museum and Library in Freemasons' Hall and all the members of Grand Lodge Staff who have assisted me in so many ways with the production of this book. My thanks, also, are due to the Members of the Robert Burns Anniversary Committee, whose assistance and support have been so much appreciated.

To all who have contributed so much to our understanding of the masonic life of the Bard, my thanks, also, are due. Without their work, and permission to reproduce it, this book could not have been completed. Worthy of special mention is Lodge Quatuor Coronati, No. 2076 (English Constitution); recognised as being the world's premier Lodge of Research.

The illustrations published within this book are reproduced by the kind permission of the Grand Lodge of Scotland, the Daughter Lodges of the Scottish Craft and the Grand Lodge of the Royal Order of Scotland (who are now the owners of St John's Chapel, the meeting place of Lodge Canongate Kilwinning, No. 2).

John Weir
Editor

FOREWORD

The Grand Lodge of Scotland had been in existence only for twenty-three years when Robert Burns was born in Alloway and in the ensuing years the poetry, songs and letters of the Poet have had a continuing attraction for people in all walks of life, and rightly so.

In commemorating the Bi-centenary of the death of Caledonia's Bard it is most appropriate that Brother John Weir should collate, in one volume, various papers and lectures concerning Robert Burns, emphasising his Masonic activities.

I would express not only my own thanks but those, also, of countless Freemasons to Brother John Weir for increasing our knowledge of one of Scotland's most famous sons.

The proceeds of the sale of 'Robert Burns – The Freemason' will benefit the Benevolent Funds of the Grand Lodge of Scotland and by purchasing this copy you may find satisfaction in knowing that the less fortunate are being assisted.

Finally, it is my very great pleasure to commend this book to you.

Edinburgh – June, 1996   Burton
                                          Grand Master Mason

INTRODUCTION

WHEN A POET'S work has been translated into at least eighteen different languages and his life and work has been the subject of over 4,000 books, it could be argued that there would be very little new left to write about such a personage. As we now approach the bi-centenary of our National Bard's death there will doubtless be many more biographical works published. Bearing this in mind, how can the Grand Lodge of Scotland possibly justify the commissioning of a new book entitled *Robert Burns – The Freemason.*

There is a very straightforward reason – the life and times of "Robert Burns – The Freemason" has not yet been fully addressed. Of course, during the past two hundred years, various Masonic scholars have written papers and delivered orations on the subject of Brother Robert Burns. Some of these works have been published in limited circulation journals, especially the Year Book of the Grand Lodge of Scotland. Never before have all these manifold thoughts and differing shades of opinion been gathered together, scrutinised, amended and issued as a comprehensive work.

The reason for the suppression of Robert Burns' detailed work for Freemasonry is best explained by the fact that most of his early biographers were not apparently Freemasons. Further, had they been so privileged to have known Brother Robert Burns to be a member of the Craft, it is most improbable that they would have revealed the fact in the 19th and 20th centuries because it was deemed advisable to be discreet about anyone's involvement.

In the late 20th century, a more liberal attitude prevails and Freemasons are now very comfortable with the statement that "Freemasonry is a Society with Secrets" rather than the Victorian concept that "Freemasonry is a Secret Society". Thus the time is right for the Grand Lodge of Scotland to undertake this important venture.

This book which has been published in June 1996 to commemorate the bi-centenary of the death of Brother Robert Burns is a compilation of many lectures and papers delivered by eminent Freemasons and, where appropriate and necessary, these have been amended to ensure their accuracy. Another purpose of this book is to resolve any uncertainties of Robert Burns' Masonic career as he travels from his Mother Lodge to Mauchline, on to Edinburgh, thence to the Borders and finally to Dumfries. In the same manner as our National Bard's original biographers caused some feathers to be ruffled by some of their outrageous claims concerning the poet's life (and many were subsequently discounted) so now this account addresses many inaccuracies with regard to his Freemasonry.

Due weight is given to the influence of Freemasonry and its precepts on the work of the poet. Conversely, it also traces the effects that his life and example had on the future of Freemasonry. Although, as already stated, some of the papers have been published for limited circulation among Freemasons, this complete work reveals much new information regarding the life of Robert Burns and, in this sense, is a welcome addition to the plethora of "Burnsiana".

In the main, the work is chronological for the subject matter lends itself to this method of arrangement, especially as the Masonic records regarding Brother

Burns are also available in this form. The work falls into four main sections, sub-divided as follows:

1. Early Masonic career – a general background to Scottish Freemasonry as it existed during Burns' lifetime.
2. As a result of the success of his Kilmarnock Edition, the poet's visits to Edinburgh, the tours of the Borders and the Highlands.
3. The latter years, dealing with the family's move to Ellisland, his increasing health problems and his untimely death.
4. The Masonic poems of Robert Burns, his life and times, are subjected to the most meticulous scrutiny by three Masonic scholars. Their Treatises relating to the Masonic writings of Robert Burns show the development of his generous guidance to all Freemasons. The section is concluded by an Appraisal of the Influence of Freemasonry on him.

When considering the publication of this book there were many occasions when one was placed in the position which the poet had faced with regard to the publication of his works. One is reminded of his reply when he was asked by a publisher to name a fee for his work. Burns replied: "To name a fee for this work would be down-right sodomy of the soul – this work I do for Scotia's sake." Such was the motivation of our National Bard, here was a man who assisted others at every possible opportunity. Of particular concern to him was the well-being of his fellow man and Freemason. Therefore it is worth repeating that the proceeds from the sale of this book will be donated to the Benevolent Funds of the Grand Lodge of Scotland. We are certain that this generous support would have met with the complete approval of our Immortal Brother.

June 1996
Edinburgh

Part One

Chapter One

EARLY FREEMASONRY IN TARBOLTON

Exactly how Freemasonry came to Tarbolton in 1771 must ever remain a matter of conjecture, as there are no records extant. Strangely enough, in a community rich in historical associations, local legends, traditions, and cherished family anecdotes, rarely are there any stories told about the origins of freemasonry in this romantic Ayrshire village or of the circumstances or motivations which culminated in an application from the Brethren – Masons in and around the village of Tarbolton – being submitted to the Kilwinning Lodge "praying the authority of the Kilwinning Lodge to be formed into a Regular Lodge or Society . . .". In a community – small though it was (population approximately 450) – which in the early 1770s could boast a Weavers' Guild, a Universal Friendly Society, a Farmers' Society, and later a Reform Movement, the formation of a Masons' Lodge would neither occasion surprise nor evoke undue comment. The villagers were accustomed to progressive movements. Tarbolton was just such a place.

Two factors which may well have contributed to the growth of freemasonry in this corner of old Strathclyde are worthy of consideration:

1. Speculative freemasonry stemmed immediately and directly from operative masonry. Stonemasonry was a prominent local craft whose craftsmen in the neighbourhood had been augmented by an influx of itinerant masons engaged in the renovation, building or re-building of the many local mansions. Indeed Rule VII (of the Early Lodge Rules) states, *inter alia,* "But if the person who wants to be made a mason has served an apprenticeship to a Mason, he shall pay only five shillings sterling, being the half of the entry money". On the 2 December, 1772 there was added the following additional rule – "That every squairsman that enters is to pay fifteen shillings sterling of entry money and everyone that is not a squairsman is to pay entry money of twenty shillings sterling." There is evidence – oral tradition – of persons being made "squaremen" and receiving the word and grip during the late 18th century at Coilsfield, near the village.

2. The sentimental deism and liberal benevolence which were the Craft's basic principles would appeal most strongly to the radically minded, independent Tarbolton weaver and to the tenant farmer.

Unfortunately the official Lodge records provide no information whatsoever on its origins. Minutes were but bald statements of election meetings with sederunts attached thereto – e.g. the following extract is typical: "Eodem die, on which day the Lodge met, there being present the following Brethren . . ." Indeed for the first few years of the Lodge's existence only the business of annual meetings is recorded and yet there is clear evidence that the Lodge was meeting regularly to enter, pass and raise candidates. Sederunts and the register of admissions are inextricably mixed and often undated. The early records, displaying an economy of words and a complete lack of feeling for history, were certainly not written with posterity in mind.

2

Be that as it may, whatever the reasons, as the first minute records:

"Tarbolton, 25 July 1771, the which day the Brethren of the Tarbolton Kilwinning Lodge having convened and after the Lodge being open by Wm. Gairdner Esqr. of Ladykirk, late Right Worshipful of Ayr Kilwinning Lodge, Grand Master, and Wm. Willson, Deputy Master of said Lodge with Wardens, Secretary, and Stewards of said Lodge received the following regulations to be engross'd into their books in order as a direction for said Lodge and are as follows viz.

FREEMASONS' RULES

I

That at the third stroke of the Grand Master's hammer, always to be repeated by the Senior Warden, there shall be a general silence . . .

II

" . . . . "

Hereafter are carefully and neatly recorded twenty-one rules which today would be regarded, *inter alia,* as a combination of Laws and Rulings, Standing Orders, a Code of Conduct, Charges and Schedules I and II. The origin of the rules is not known but they clearly follow some ancient pattern. Interestingly and quaintly worded they give an insight into social customs and styles of life of that time. Furthermore the minutes of Lodge St David's 174, – now No. 133 – constituted under Charter from the Grand Lodge on 5 February 1773, records nineteen rules which are virtually the same even to the inclusion of the following:

"Whoever shall break a drinking glass at any meeting he shall immediately pay sixpence sterling for every one he breaks before he be allowed to leave the room or company."

It was indeed a convivial, hard-drinking age!

No mere lip service was paid to the Rules. Members were frequently reminded of their obligations. Reported breaches were investigated and on occasion guilty parties disciplined. Three examples are worth quoting:

1. As an addendum to the Rules is the following minute written by John Wilson (Dr Hornbook) and signed by Burns as Depute Master: "Tarbolton Dec. 7 1785. The Lodge thought proper to commit to writing that old regulation that whoever stands as Master shall be bound, at the entry of a new member, for that member's dues if the money is not paid or security such as the Lodge shall approve of given."

2. Burns' rhyming epistle to Dr Mackenzie, Mauchline – "Friday first's the day appointed/by the Right Worshipful annointed/To hold our grand procession" is more than an invitation to the annual meeting. It is a telling reminder of the good Doctor's obligation in terms of Rule XIII.

3. "Tarbolton 2 Dec. 1789 . . . They next proceeded to make enquiry into Brother McDonald's conduct at a former meeting which had been found great fault with as Senior Warden and excluded him unanimously from that office and elected Bro. Hugh Manson in his place till the 24 June next."

But to return to the first minute – after a formal signing of the Freemasons' Rules the Brethren were joined by the R.W. Dr John Nimmo, Grand Master of the Ayr Kilwinning Lodge, who presented the Charter from the Kilwinning Lodge, dated 17 May 1771. The Lodge is still in possession of the Kilwinning Charter. The minute continues:

". . . Thereafter the said Charter was openly read and after prayer by Rev Mr Widrow, one of the Brethren, and a charge by Bro. Alex Gillies of the Kilwinning Lodge, the same was consecrated in ample form and full powers given to them as to any other Lodges as are consecrating the same: Thereafter out of the members of the said Tarbolton Kilwinning Lodge the officers are elected and are, viz:

1. Alex Montgomerie, Esq. of Coilsfield – Grand Master
2. John Hood in Tarbolton – D.M.
3. John Anderson, mason at Adam Town Burn – S.W.
4. Alex Wilson – J.W.
5. (name omitted) – Treasurer
6. John McLatchie, innkeeper at Tarbolton – Secretary
7. W. Anderson – S.S.
8. Adam Grieve – J.S.
9. John Mitchell – Standard Bearer
10. Matthew Wilson – Tyler

The above to continue in their offices for the ensuing year who all have accepted the same and given their oaths de fideli. John Nimmo, G.M."

The minute has been signed by Wm. Gairdner, Wm. Willson, the Wardens, Secretary, and Stewards of Lodge Ayr Kilwinning who had constituted the Lodge at the opening ceremony and by Alex Montgomerie and John Hood, G.M. and D.M., of the newly consecrated Tarbolton Kilwinning Lodge. On the adjoining page are appended the signatures of 63 Brethren who attended. Some of these Brethren were to figure prominently in the subsequent history of the Lodge: e.g. Jas. Dalrymple (of Orangefield), John Hamilton (of Sundrum), Thos. Wallace Dunlop (of Craigie), John Andrew, John Dove, James Manson, John Richard, Hume Campbell, John Rankin, John Ferguson and Henry Cowan. Thus did Freemasonry come to this ancient Burgh of Barony. What hopes the founder members entertained for their Lodge can only be guessed. They were not to know then that within a decade history would be made in the village and the name of "Auld Tarbowtin" for ever assured. This, unfortunately, was not to be achieved without dissension, turbulence, and bitter animosities.

Within two years the Scottish passion for schism betrayed itself. On 5 February 1773 the Grand Lodge of Scotland considered a petition on behalf of Sir Thomas Wallace Dunlop Bart. and ten others, all members of Lodge Tarbolton Kilwinning "setting forth that **they being at a distance from their Mother Lodges** (the bold is the present author's) nevertheless were willing to promote Masonry in the place above mentioned and craved to hold under the sanction of Grand Lodge . . . and praying the Grand Lodge to grant them a Charter of Erection and constitution for a Free Mason Lodge to be held in the Town or Village of Tarbolton by the name and Title of Tarbolton Saint David's . . ."

Grand Lodge accepted the petition and as the first minute of Lodge St David records: "1773 Feb. 26 was the day of the Charter of St David's Lodge being granted in faiver of Sir Thomas Walles Bart., John Mitchell . . ." (Sir Thomas Wallace Dunlop Bart., second son of John Dunlop of Dunlop House and Frances Ann Wallace – the Mrs Dunlop, friend and correspondent of Burns – succeeded to the title in 1771 and assumed the Wallace family name). Harvey in his book, *Robt. Burns as a Freemason,* a work which in relation to Tarbolton contains several gross inaccuracies, seeking to justify the schism, maintains that – "the influence of Kilwinning at this time was rapidly waning before the growing power of the Grand Lodge of Scotland." Others, since, have reiterated, parrot-wise, his conclusion

4

and would attribute to the founder members of St David qualities of prescience which they themselves would never have claimed. This is too simplistic. The credulity of those who have supported this theory is matched only by their naivety. Such an approach displays a total lack of knowledge of the vagaries of village life and completely underestimates the power and influence that Lodge Mother Kilwinning continued to exert, not only in Ayrshire but in the whole West of Scotland and far beyond during the next 30 years, a power and influence which enabled her to rejoin Grand Lodge in 1807 largely on terms of her own dictating. For the most part, for the majority of Brethren in the village at that time, Grand Lodge was an irrelevance. Then, and for many years to come, her control was so lax and ineffectual as to be of little or no consequence. The real reason for the secession resided, as has already been stated, in the Scottish propensity for schism and in all probability sprang from local differences, petty jealousies or unsatisfied ambitions. Hans Hecht, in his *Robert Burns, The Man and His Work*, hits the nail on the head when he attributes the secession to "internal friction". No reference, whatsoever, is made in the minutes of Lodge Tarbolton Kilwinning to the secession. Nevertheless, within a year the Brethren of Tarbolton Kilwinning, no doubt to safeguard their position and perhaps as a precaution, applied for a Charter from Grand Lodge. The Lodge minute, worthy of note, is quoted at length:

"On the 24 June 1774, this being St John the Baptist's Day and the anniversary meeting of Tarbolton Kilwinning Lodge . . . the Lodge was opened in due form and there was presented and read the Charter for said Brethren from the Grand Lodge of Scotland, bearing the date 27 May 1774 under the stile and Title of St James Tarbolton Kilwinning Lodge No. 178 . . . . The Brethren then marched in due and orderly procession from their Lodge Room to the Church where an excellent sermon was preached from the text Romans 12 verses 9–11 by the Parish Minister Bro. Rev P. Wodrow. The Brethren returned from Church in the same due and orderly procession to their Lodge Room and after prayer by Bro. Wodrow proceeded to the election of Office Bearers for the ensuing year, when by plurality of votes they made choice of the following worthy Br. into their respective offices – viz: James Montgomery Esqr. – G.M. etc."

The other office bearers are listed and 43 names are appended to the minute. This account of the early history of the Lodge may seem somewhat excessive but is deliberate in order to dispel doubts and to correct the many inaccuracies which, over the years, have appeared in print from a variety of sources. Two Lodges, both operating under Grand Lodge Charters, now functioned in the village and for the next seven years continued to co-exist with considerable success and in close harmony. It is surely a tribute to both Lodges that from their original formation until 1780 each had initiated upwards of 140 members. Many prominent members of the community were associated with both Lodges. Despite this initial success it became increasingly apparent that a small community could not continue adequately to sustain two active Lodges. Oblique references indicate a growing desire to establish a single Lodge in the village.

The initial overtures regarding a possible union (Juncheon) emanated from Lodge St David. Its minute of the quarterly meeting of 6 December 1780, when 17 members attended, records what is virtually a notice of motion by Brothers Henry Cowan and John Richard "that the sense of the Lodge re a proposed union with Lodge St James may be given pro. and con. on the first Wednesday of May 1781."

On 6 June 1781 the Lodge St David minute records, *inter alia*, "have considered on our offers to St James Lodge respecting a Juncheon on the 24th – i.e. the anniversary meeting of both lodges – also their answer and find by a majority of votes both lodges may unite on terms offered and exchanged this day".

On 25 June 1781 the two lodges were united under the style and title of St David. The minute of Lodge St David is as follows:

"Sederunt for June 25 1781. On the above mentioned day the two lodges formerly going under the names of St James and St Davids were united and now go under the name of St Davids being the oldest Charter and made choice of the following office bearers. List of Office Bearers for 1781."

The Choice of office bearers had been made with discretion. It was a judicious sharing of offices from members of each lodge. Joseph Norman, a Past Master of St David was chosen as Master. Geo. Guthrie – Senior Warden (St David), John Highet – Junior Warden (St James), James Manson – Treasurer (St James), Robt. Wodrow – Secretary (St James), Wm. Corbett – Depute Master (St James). Thereafter each office has two Brethren, one from each lodge, and finally a Senior and a Junior Tyler. Not unexpectedly, there is no reference in the St James minute book to the union.

The minutes of 4 July – the first meeting thereafter of the united lodge – and 1 October 1781, as recorded in the St David minute book are historic and are here stated in full:

"Sederunt for July 4th. Robt. Burns in Lochly was entered an apprentice. Joph. Norman, M."

"Sederunt October 1st 1781. Robt. Burns in Lochly was passed and raised. Henry Cowan being Master, James Humphrey being Senr. Warden and Alex Smith Junr. Do., Robt. Wodrow Secy. and Jas. Manson, Treasurer and John Tannock Taylor and others of the Brethren being present."

It should be noted that the first three Brethren mentioned were not elected office bearers and accordingly must have been acting for the evening. the elected Master, Joseph Norman, has signed the minute.

The union was ill-fated. By 5 December 1781, the date of the next meeting, dissension had arisen. Robt. Wodrow, the elected Secretary of St David, had removed from the Lodge Charter Chest the Charter, Books, and sundry papers belonging to St James, for which act he was, by decision of the meeting of 24 June 1782, expunged from Lodge St David and the Master and Wardens were ordained and appointed to prosecute him. Later Robert Wodrow became Secretary and in 1810 Master of the re-constituted St James. The office bearers of St David embittered by the resumption of St James, petitioned the Sheriff of Ayr to grant a warrant to apprehend Wodrow. Rejecting the Sheriff's findings, they authorised the Master and Wardens or their successors in office to prosecute Wodrow before the Court of Session or by appeal to the Grand Lodge. The Lodge retained, through Robertson Smith, Writers in Ayr, Brother David Cathcart, Greenfield, Alloway, an advocate – Brother Cathcart later became Lord of Session with the legal title of Lord Alloway – to act for the Lodge in the dispute.

The minutes, recorded in great detail, indicate not merely the depth of feeling engendered but literally how obsessed the office bearers had become with the issue. For six years it was the major lodge business. Their obsession became counter-productive and indeed marks the turning point in the history of Lodge St David. It was the beginning of the end. Throughout, Wodrow remained defiant. Even the order from Grand Lodge anent restoration of the documents failed to move him. The minute of Lodge St James is brief and to the point: "Tarbolton 17 June 1782. St James's Lodge met upon the same footing that it was before the Juncheon. Jas. Montgomerie, G.M. for the night."

On 8 July 1782 they re-constituted the Lodge and on 8 August 1782 elected a full quota of office bearers for the ensuing year. The only other reference to the unhappy events of 1781 appears in the minute of 1 June 1785 when the thanks of the Lodge were unanimously voted to Captn. Montgomerie, the Right Worshipful Master of the Lodge, "for his trouble in recovering their colours for some time illegally retained by the Lodge of St David".

Robert Burns – the only person to be initiated and later passed and raised in the united lodge – associated himself with the reformed St James, became a most active member, and from 1784 to 1788 was Depute Master and, as such, was "oft honour'd with supreme command". Burns proved himself not only a most enthusiastic freemason but a most competent Depute Master. During this period the Lodge met with increased frequency both in the village and in neighbouring communities. For example, the Lodge, or a deputation from the Lodge, met regularly at Mauchline and on one occasion, 5 October 1786, with Burns in the chair at Sorn. It is also to be noted that at one such meeting of the deputation at Mauchline Gilbert Burns, the poet's brother, was enter'd, passed and raised. Later in his capacity as Junior Warden Gilbert was to preside, on at least four occasions, over meetings of the deputation in Mauchline. Again, at the lodge meeting in Mauchline on 25 July 1787, with the poet presiding, Professor Dugald Stewart of Catrine, Claude Alexander of Ballochmyle, Claud Wilson of Paisley, John Farquhar Gray of Gilmilnscroft and Dr George Grierson of Glasgow were admitted Honorary Members of the Lodge.

The Lodge greatly valued the importance of its Mauchline connection. On 3 December 1788 it was agreed, on representation, from the Mauchline deputation "that the office bearers with as many of the Brethren as shall think proper shall go from this place to Mauchline with the colour and insignia of the Lodge for the purpose of having a procession there and dinner at John Dove's upon Monday 12 Jan. first" Again on the occasion of the annual meeting on 24 June 1790 it was proposed "that there should be an Annual Meeting of the Lodge once every two years at Mauchline. But this being ags. [against] the original institution of this Lodge to have an annual meeting anywhere but at Tarbolton, the seat of the Lodge, this proposal was refused by a great majority. But as the interest of the lodge has been much advanced by a number of worthy members in and around Mauchline who have joined it the Lodge agreed to have a general meeting at Mauchline some time in December next – the day to be fixed afterward." No such meeting ever took place. Incidentally, the following year 1791 Lodge St Mungo (now dormant) was chartered in Mauchline.

The Burns period in the history of the Lodge had been a hectic one. He had a real zest for freemasonry. He clearly appreciated that true masonic fellowship is intimately bound up with the company of one's brethren and cannot be dissociated from the lodge room. Hence the frequency of meetings under his direction. While it is true that in the immediate post-Burns period lodge meetings were less frequent we must not jump to conclusions, as so many chroniclers have done, and assume that, bereft of the personality, zeal and driving force of the poet, there was a gradual diminution of interest in the Lodge and its activities. This was just not so. The availability of candidates from the village and its immediate neighbourhood was closely related to the size of the male population. Some decline was inevitable – in a small community the number of candidates is limited – but 56 candidates in the ten years from 1790-1799 was not insignificant and, as we shall observe presently, other horizons beckoned.

Chapter Two

BURNS AND THE TARBOLTON FREEMASONS

Because of its close association with our National Bard, Lodge St James possesses a number of interesting and valuable relics of the Burns period. These include:

1. The Minute Book, Ledgers and Roll Books of the Lodge from its inception but especially the first, covering the years 1771-1790. In it is recorded in full Burns' active association with Lodge St James, particularly noteworthy his period as Depute Master, 1784-88. Three minutes were written in full by the poet, the first being unsigned. In all he has signed the minutes on 32 occasions. The poet's brother, Gilbert, has signed the minutes on five occasions, one of the minutes being written in full by him. In addition there are minutes written by John Wilson (Dr Hornbook) as Secretary. Two minutes have also been signed by him as Master *pro. tem.*

2. The Minute Books of Lodge St David from 1773 to 1843 when the Lodge was disbanded. Previous reference has been made to the entries relating to Burns' entering, passing and raising. These Minute Books, after the dissolution of the Lodge in 1843 became the property of the Oliver family and were handed down in the families of their descendants as treasured heirlooms. On 28 May 1920 Mrs Murchie indicated her desire to dispose of the Minute Books. On the advice of Provincial Grand Lodge a deputation from St James met with her but failed to persuade her to "hand them over". On 8 June 1923 representatives of St James discussed the situation with representatives of Provincial Grand Lodge and the Master and Secretary of Lodge St David (Tarbolton) Mauchline No. 133. Their final decision was to refer the whole matter to Grand Lodge. On 3 October 1924 Provincial Grand Secretary intimated to the parties the opinion of Grand Lodge. It was further agreed to initiate legal proceedings to recover the Minute Books. This process was unsuccessful as the terms of the final minute of 7 January 1843 were held to give possession of the lodge funds and property to eight remaining members and their heirs. The Minute Books passed from Mrs Murchie, Burns Tavern, to her daughter Grace, Mrs Stewart, Black Bull Hotel, Mauchline and in time to her daughter, Olive. On 30 November 1970 they were auctioned in Sotheby's, London. Lodge St James learned of this from Grand Secretary, Brother Dr Alex Buchan, via our own Immediate Past Provincial Grand Master, Brother T. Muir Wilson. At a hastily convened meeting the office bearers commissioned Brother Muir Wilson, who had placed his services at the disposal of the Lodge, to endeavour to purchase the books for St James. This was happily effected, the Minute Books being bought for £500. It must be placed on record, however, that such was the determination of the office bearers, with the concurrence of the Brethren, to secure such valuable records for Lodge St James No. 135 that even if the price had been doubled the Minute Books would still have come to Tarbolton. When Brother Horace W. McCurdy, George Washington Lodge No. 251, an Honorary Member of No. 135 and a generous benefactor of the Lodge, learned of the purchase he refunded the total cost. The Books are, therefore, recognised as a gift to the Lodge from Brother McCurdy.

3. The first office bearers' jewels presented by Captain James Montgomerie, Master in 1774. In "The Farewell to the Brethren of Lodge St James" Burns makes special reference to the Master and the Master's Jewel: "And you, farewell! whose merits claim Justly, that Highest Badge to wear."

4. The Master's Chair and Footstool.

5. The Candlesticks and Snuffer.

6. The Depute Master's Apron worn by Burns.

7. The Bible bought by Burns with Lodge money, and Square and Compasses purchased for the Lodge by Brother McDonald, Secretary.

8. The clock hammer and pendulum of the Kirk clock: "The Auld Kirk-hammer struck the bell."

9. The copper plate from which were printed the summonses to meetings issued to Brethren. The practice of issuing these summonses has had, of necessity, been discontinued. Each initiate receives one "as a souvenir of a most important occasion".

10. The Lodge Snuff Box which the last real snuff taker in the village, Brother Matthew T. Wilson, Master 1924-25, kept constantly filled.

11. The letter sent to the Lodge by Burns from Edinburgh, dated 23 August 1787. At that time in the absence of convenient banking facilities – the Lodge did not open a bank account until 18 January 1817 partly, no doubt, because of inconvenience and probably because of lack of confidence in banks – the Lodge loaned its available capital to Brethren at 5% p.a. interest. Quarterly meetings were "settling days". On occasion, depending on the state of trade in the village, Brethren

defaulted or "craved days". Defaulters were liable to prosecution. In this letter, which contained an apology for absence, Burns is interceding on behalf of defaulters, hence his comment: "If you please, I wish you would delay prosecuting defaulters till I come home . . . and those who confess debt and crave days, I think we should spare them. Farewell!" He then added the famous stanza beginning:

"Within your dear mansion may wayward contention
Or wither'd envy ne'er enter."

It is interesting to record that at the quarterly meeting, 5 September 1787, the office bearers agreed to defer the prosecution of them until the next meeting.

12. The signatures of the three sons of the Poet viz: Robt. Burns, Wm. Nicol Burns, James Glencairn Burns.

13. The Tracing Boards – cloth and canvas – used in the Lodge at the time of Burns. These old Tracing Boards were, on 7 May 1920, returned to the Lodge beautifully renovated and in handsome frames by the Brethren of Lodge Wishaw St Mary No. 31. This had been executed by members of a deputation of Lodge St Mary who had previously visited Tarbolton and had expressed a desire to leave something to commemorate their visit. They asked to be allowed to take away the old Tracing Boards and have them renovated to preserve them.

14. The veritable mallet used by Burns, and proudly by all his successors, when presiding over the Lodge.

This is a wonderful heritage of which the Brethren of St James are justly proud. Here we have a unique collection of relics pertaining to Burns' masonic connections with Tarbolton. With the exception of the Tyler's Sword of Lodge St David and the Peggy Orr, Toddy Bowl and Jug, both in the Bachelors' Club, Tarbolton, two Candlesticks belonging to St David, still in private hands, and a small piece of silk ($1/2$in square) cut from the Burns apron, now in the Lodge of Robert Burns, Australia, on the authority of Mr John Hunter, a direct descendant of John Richard, and who as a boy spent his holidays in the "Bachelors' Club", there are no other authentic relics of this period of the Poet's Masonic life now in existence. The chairs of Lodge St David were disposed of because, as the minute of 24 June 1837 states, "they were rotting". With the passage of time other articles, documents, etc., met the same fate as that which befell the Depute Master's chair of

The above contains a full minute, written and signed by Gilbert Burns; also a full minute, written and signed by Robert Burns; and Burns' signature to another minute.

11

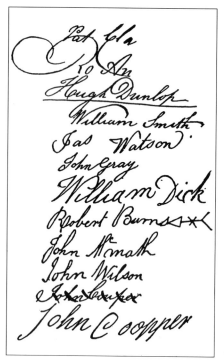

Above contains the signature of the Poet, with his Mason's Mark (nine points); also the signature of John Wilson (Dr Hornbook).

Lodge St James after the Burns Centenary Exhibition in Glasgow 1896 – consigned to the flames – while the mallet and certain papers (copies of diplomas?), handed down as treasured possessions in the Cowan and John Richard families, were destroyed in the disastrous fire which gutted the home of Mrs John Richard, who sadly lost her life in the fire – 2 October 1915. (Mrs Richard was the second wife of John Richard who pre-deceased her in 1912. His first wife, Elizabeth Cowan was the grand-daughter of Henry Cowan who occupied the chair on the evening Burns was passed and raised.)

In June 1890 Brother Peter Watson, Lodge St James, No. 135 contributed four articles on Robert Burns to the *Kilmarnock Standard*, entitled "Burns' Association with the Tarbolton Freemasons".

It seems most appropriate at this stage to quote Brother Watson's detailed account of the Minutes of Burns' full term as Depute Master – 1784-1788.

We further quote from the late Mr Watson's articles:

Burns must have been the life and soul of the St James Lodge in more ways than one. The minutes show that there were more meetings when he was an office-bearer than at any other period. Though Burns is known to have been a member from the end of 1781, it is not till 27th July, 1784, that we have the record of his appointment to office in the lodge.

Right contains the calligraphy of John Wilson (Dr Hornbook), the secretary of the lodge, and a full minute, written and signed by Burns.

> Br James Manson Treasurer
> Br John Manson Senior Stewart
> B: John Cunninghame Junior Stewart
> B: John Dunnock Pass Master
> Br James McWhinnie Tyler
>
> Tarbolton June 23d 1786. —
> This night the Lodge met, and Robt Indrew a Brother of St David's Tarbolton, was admitted by unanimous vote, gratis likewise James Good having been duely recommended was entered an Apprentice. —
>
> Ro. Burns Dm

The Deputy Mastership was then conferred upon him – a position that carried with it the active duties of the Master, who was seldom present at the meetings. All assemblies at which the Master was not present were under the presidency of the Deputy Master, and it is in this capacity that Burns has signed so many of the minutes. There are three short minutes written in full by the Poet. The first is dated "Tarbolton, 1st September, 1784," but is unsigned, a circumstance not uncommon amongst the records of that time. This minute bears marks of literary conceit at any rate, the antithesis being worthy of note. It is almost ludicrous to find the world famed Poet thus writing:

"This night the lodge met, and ordered four pounds of candles and one quire of eight pence paper for the use of the lodge, which money was laid out by the treasurer, and the candles and paper laid in accordingly."

The other minutes, written fully in the Poet's hand, are as follows:
"Tarbolton, 23rd June, 1786. – This night the lodge met, and Robert Andrew, a broth-er of St David's, Tarbolton, was admitted by unanimous vote, gratis: likewise James Good, having been duly recommended, was entered an apprentice.

R. BURNS, D.M."

"Tarbolton, 18th August (no year, but from the dates immediately before and after, sure to be 1786). – This night the lodge met, and James Tennant, from Ochiltree, having been recommended, was admitted accordingly.

Robt. BURNS, D.M."

It is a curious coincidence that two of the three minutes written in full by Robert Burns are near to the one written in the hand of Gilbert Burns, the three being in view at the one opening of the book. Burns, who, whether living at Lochlea or Mossgiel, must have had several miles to walk in order to attend the meetings of the lodge, was most attentive to his duties. The first minute which he signed as Depute Master is dated 29th June, 1785, and the last to which his name is adhibited is dated 23rd May, 1788; but this does not mark his final departure from the lodge, as Dr Robert Chambers erroneously states in his "Land of Burns". On 21st October, 1788, and again on 11th November of the same year, the minutes record that Brother Robert Burns was in the chair, though his signature is not attached. Both of these meetings took place at Mauchline, and they must have been held during a flying visit from Ellisland, as Burns settled there on 12th June, 1788, a letter of his, dated 13th June, stating that "this is the second day" he had been on his farm in Dumfriesshire. Between the first and the last signatures, Burns has in all signed his name twenty-nine times, and on one occasion he has his initials placed to a postscript; but one of the signatures has been cut out by some unscrupulous admirer. The theft occurs in the second last minute that was signed by the Poet, the signature being that of the main part of the minute – the minute having been divided into three. Burns has signed a "P.S." to the same minute, and also an addition to this "P.S." connected by the words "also at same time," and to the last of these hangs a tale. The gentleman in Tarbolton , who had charge of the minute book was at one time showing it to a visitor, but, being called away for a moment to attend a sick daughter in another room, the visitor and the book were left unwatched. After the visitor departed, the gentleman was asked by his daughter to look at the book, as she was afraid something would be found wrong. Whilst her father was with her, she heard either a knife or a pair of scissors at work, and she was right in the surmise that one of the minutes had been tampered with. On discovering this, the visitor was communicated with, and ordered to return the stolen property or suffer the conse-quences, and the cutting was returned. The stolen part is now neatly pasted in its original place, and, being on the opposite page from the blank left by the cut out signature, elo-quent testimony is borne to the rapacity of collectors, and the value placed upon relics of our National Bard. Strange as the omission may appear, there is no mention in the min-utes of the Poet's demission of office, nor of his leaving the district, even though Burns himself looked so favourably on the position he held amongst the Tarbolton Masons as to address a poem to them as his farewell. This was in 1786, when he seriously contem-

13

plated emigrating to the West Indies. It is curious also to note the manner in which Burns signs his name; in this there is great variety. In regard to the spelling, he continues the "Burness" up till 1st March, 1786 – the first under the more familiar "Burns" being of date 25th May of the same year. Whilst Burns signs "Burness" so long, it is noteworthy that the references to him in the text of the minutes are always spelt "Burns," except on one occasion, when the name had first been spelt "Burns," but afterwards altered to "Burness," probably by the Poet himself, or at least by his instructions, as his name appears at the foot of this minute as "Burness." In regard to the Christian name, it appears once before Burness as "Robert," and thirteen times it precedes the same spelling as "Robt.". Before the later spelling of "Burns" we have it once only in full as "Robert," a single time as "R," and eleven times as "Robt." – this latter having, it is thus seen, the greatest favour with the Poet. Amongst a long list of signatures of members, many of them having their Mason's marks attached, we find Burns signing himself in full, "Robert Burns," and adding his masonic mark of nine points in the same line. This signature has less resemblance to the familiar and undoubtedly genuine form than any of the others, but there is no date to it, and it is just possible that the conditions under which he signed were what the lodge might term "unfortunate."

Burns' younger brother, Gilbert, was entered, passed, and raised as a brother on 1st March, 1786 (the last date on which the Poet signed Burness), and must, for a time at least, have taken an active part in the affairs of the lodge. We find Gilbert signing the minutes on five separate occasions between 11th December, 1786 and 21st December, 1787, one of these, as already said, being written by him in full. The last references to either of the brothers occur on 18th November and 20th November, 1788, on which dates the text of the minutes states that Brother Gilbert Burns occupied the chair. These last-named meetings were held in Mauchline, and form the closing testimony to the warm interest maintained for six or seven years by Robert, and the shorter period by Gilbert, in the affairs of St James (Tarbolton) Lodge.

Burns signs the minute relating to the visit of Professor Dugald Stewart to the lodge, who at that time was tenant of Catrine House, and was a friend of the Poet. The record is as follows:

"A deputation of the lodge met at Mauchline on 25th July, 1787, and entered Brother Alexander Allison of Barmuir as apprentice. Likewise admitted Brothers Professor Stewart of Catrine; and Claud Alexander, Esq., of Ballochmyle; Claud Neilson, Esq., Paisley; John Farquhar Gray, Esq., of Gilmilnscroft; and Dr George Grierson, Glasgow, honorary members of this lodge," the minute being signed "Robt. Burns, D.M." (in very faint ink).

John Wilson, who was parish teacher of Tarbolton, and the Dr Hornbook of Burns's well known poem, was secretary to the lodge from 8th August, 1782, till some time in 1787, and in that capacity wrote many of the minutes. Two of them are signed by him – one as "Master *pro tempore,*" and the other as "M.P.T." This last minute shows his adhesion to the lodge after his successor in the secretaryship had been appointed, and it is not shown that he was at the date the holder of any office other than that of ordinary membership. Immediately succeeding Wilson's first signature as "Master pro tempore," he finds an imitator in James M'Donald, the succeeding chairman, who signs his name, and adds "P.T." merely, a thing that occurs also once afterwards in the writing of another temporary president.

Two of the Grand Masters sign the minutes occasionally viz., Mr James Montgomerie of Coilsfield, and Mr James Dalrymple of Orangefield, but these are the only names adhibited of the half-dozen Grand Masters who held office during the years embraced in the minutes. The others were Mr John Hamilton of Sundrum – a name still honoured in the county in the person of the present proprietor; Mr Mungo Smith of Drongan; Mr Alex Montgomerie of Coilsfield (a branch of the Eglinton family,); and Mr Gavin Hamilton, the well known friend and correspondent of Burns. The name of the Montgomeries suggests the immortality shed upon the family and their estate by the Poet's works. The gratitude of the lodge is expressed at one meeting to Captain Montgomerie, the Right Worshipful Master of the lodge, for his trouble in recovering their colours, "for some time illegally retained by the Lodge of St David."

On 27 March 1786, the Poet was admitted a member of Lodge Loudoun (Kilwinning), Newmilns, of which his friend, Gavin Hamilton, was at that time Master. On 26 October of the same year he was made an honorary member of Lodge St John (Kilwinning), Kilmarnock.

Passing from Lodge St James, it is now well known that, until the close of his career, the Poet manifested a warm interest in Freemasonry. It is easy to imagine what a charm he lent to the various meetings he attended.

Lodge St James, to which the Poet addressed his pathetic "Farewell," is the proud possessor of various valuable relics – Burns' chair, mallet, and Bible; the jewels which as Depute Master he wore; his apron (all tattered and torn); the old Minute Book, in which, as already mentioned, his handwriting frequently appears; also the original of the kindly letter which he sent from Edinburgh to the Lodge, which then met in Manson's Inn.

The letter, dated 23 August, 1787, is in the following terms:

MEN AND BRETHREN, – I am truly sorry it is not in my power to be at your quarterly meeting. If I must be absent in body, believe me I shall be present in spirit. I suppose those who owe us moneys, by bill or otherwise, will appear – I mean those we summoned. If you please, I wish you would delay prosecuting defaulters till I come home. The Court is up, and I will be home before it sits down. In the meantime, to take a note of who appear, and who do not, of our faulty debtors, will be right in my opinion; and those who confess debt and crave days, I think we should spare them. Farewell!

> Within your dear mansion may wayward contention
>   Or wither'd envy ne'er enter,
> May secrecy round by the mystical bound,
>   And brotherly love be the centre.

This stanza might serve as a Masonic motto all the world over.

The Masonic interest in *The Farewell* is so great as to justify its reproduction:

The Farewell

> Adieu! a heart-warm fond adieu!
>   Dear brothers of the mystic tie!
> Ye favour'd ye enlighten'd few,
>   Companions of my social joy!
> Tho' I to foreign lands must hie,
>   Pursuing Fortune's slidd'ry ba',
> With melting heart, and brimful eye,
>   I'll mind you still, tho' far awa'.
>
> Oft have I met your social band,
>   And spent the cheerful festive night;
> Oft, honour'd with supreme command,
>   Presided o'er the sons of light:
> And by that hieroglyphic bright,
>   Which none but craftsmen ever saw!
> Strong memory on my heart shall write
>   Those happy scenes when far awa'!

May freedom, harmony, and love
    Unite you in the grand design,
Beneath th' Omniscient eye above,
    The glorious Architect Divine!
That you may keep th' unerring line,
    Still rising by the plummet's law,
Till Order bright completely shine,
    Shall be my pray'r when far awa'.

And You, farewell! whose merits claim,
    Justly, that highest badge to wear!
Heav'n bless your honour'd noble name,
    To Masonry and Scotia dear!
A last request permit me here:
    When yearly ye assemble a', –
One round, I ask it with a tear,
To him, the Bard that's far awa'.

Chapter Three

BURNS, THE YOUNG FREEMASON

(Address delivered by Brother John Weir in Lodge St James Tarbolton Kilwinning, No. 135, on 4 July 1981 on the occasion of the celebration of the bi-centenary of the initiation of Robert Burns into Freemasonry.)

When the Right Worshipful Master invited me to propose the Toast this evening he made one condition: "I want something Masonic." I readily agreed because this is a great Masonic occasion. But, brethren, I have not interpreted my remit as being merely to recount Burns' active participation in Lodge activities. Others, over the years, have done just that: e.g. Brother Rev J. C. Higgins, P.M., did it over fifty years ago in an appendix to his admirable biography of the poet; Harvey and Halliday have given detailed accounts, although it must be said in their treatment of the Tarbolton period there are many gross inaccuracies; more recently in his article in the 1980 Year Book my old friend the late Brother Fred Belford perpetuated the errors.

These misrepresentations, what I term these stupid pinpricks of idiocy, are not deliberate. They have arisen because the authors did not know the village, its features, its associations, its traditions, its people, and they never had direct access to our Minutes. It is mere conjecture, with opinions masquerading as facts.

Marshall in his A *Winter in Edinburgh* deals with that period, but it is largely myth. And, although the poet held office in Dumfries, he was too preoccupied with his work, his poetical contribution to Johnson and, latterly, too dogged by increasing ill-health to play an active part in the affairs of his Lodge. Consequently since his active Masonic career was spent here in this village, among the brethren of this village, and in particular in this Lodge, it seemed to me appropriate that we should, on this memorable commemorative occasion, speak of "Burns, the young Freemason".

Burns became a Freemason here in this village:

> "In yon wee hoose that stauns doon by
> Masonic light fell frae on high
> Ae nicht in 'Auld Tarbowtin'."

Indeed, masonically, Burns and "Auld Tarbowtin" are synonymous. But what kind of place was Tarbolton 200 years ago?

In 1781 Tarbolton was a small rural community with a population of approximately 450 inhabitants – a population comprising weavers, stocking-makers, rural craftsmen, stone masons, wrights, millers, farriers, small farmers, agricultural workers, drainers, dykers, etc., men and women in domestic service, coachmen, gardeners, gamekeepers, etc., and all the associated services – flesher, baker, general merchant, innkeeper. The professions were represented by the ministers, the dominie, the factor, and exercising a benevolent oversight were the country lairds.

It was a village whose people took a deep, active and intelligent interest in the political, economic and religious issues of the day; a village whose people were most articulate; a village which in addition to its annually elected Burgh Council could boast a Weavers' Guild, a Farmers' Society, a Universal Friendly Society and later a Reform Movement; a village whose people were deeply religious, strongly independent and decidedly radical.

Ten years earlier, in 1771, Freemasonry had come to this village, to this ancient Burgh or Barony. Between 1771 and 1781 despite internal friction, dissensions (mainly stemming from Kirk disputes) and schisms, Freemasonry had flourished. Indeed Tarbolton could be said to have become a stronghold of Masonry.

It was into this community, with all its associations, all its traditions, all its activities, that the Burns family moved at Whitsun 1777. It was in the activities of this community that the young, impressionable Burns began to participate. It was in this community that the young Burns began to meet and associate freely with Freemasons. It was in this community, among the Brethren of this community, that as the Minute records: "Robt. Burns in Lochly was entered an apprentice."

Was it inevitable that Burns became a Freemason? Men come to Masonry from all walks of life, at different ages, and from different motivations.

What moved Burns?

1. His near neighbours, rural craftsmen, and farming associates, were Freemasons. Adam Grieve of Boghead, John Rankin of Adamhill, John Lees of Millburn, John Andrew of Fail, Samson, the Seedsman of Kilmarnock, etc.

2. His minister, Woodrow, and his assistant, McMath, were Freemasons.

3. His closest friends with whom he had formed the Bachelors' Club: Hugh Reid, Alex Brown, Walter Mitchell, Thomas Wright and Willie McGavin were active Freemasons.

4. Burns was a social being. He craved companionship. He recognised and appreciated that his friends were enjoying a fellowship denied to him and he wanted to be part of it, and;

5. A more personal and perhaps selfish reason – he was about to embark upon the Irvine project (to learn flax-dressing) and he no doubt felt that among strangers "doors would be opened".

On 4 July 1781 Burns was initiated in a Lodge which could boast three Charters: the Kilwinning Charter, the Grand Lodge Charter of St James and the Grand Lodge Charter of St David. (Burns was the only initiate of the recently combined village Lodge.)

Important though that step was, what was far more important was the fact that Burns stayed in Masonry and became an active, dedicated Freemason.

What were the salient features that rooted him to Freemasonry?

1. For him masonry was a moving, stimulating experience.

2. The basic principles of masonry appealed strongly to him.

3. He valued the companionship of masonry. He found that masonic fellowship was intimately bound up with the company of his brethren and could in no way be disassociated from the Lodge room. Hence the frequency of meetings during his four years as our Depute Master. Hence the period of masonic missionary enterprise under his leadership.

4. It brought him many influential friends – most important for an emerging poet. Indeed the masonic atmosphere strongly influenced his later life – so many of his patrons, associates, correspondents and companions were linked in our mystic chain, that bond of union, cemented here in Tarbolton.

*Outside the Bachelors' Club where Robert Burns was initiated – photograph
taken in 1982.*
*From left to right: Brother E. Stuart Falconer, Grand Secretary; Brother George
L. McGinn, Depute Provincial Grand Master of Ayrshire; Brother Sir James
Wilson McKay, The Grand Master Mason; Brother David W. Auld, Master of
Lodge St James (Kilwinning) No. 135, Tarbolton; Brother the Earl of Elgin and
Kincardine, Past Grand Master; Brother Gregor Grant, Past Substitute Grand
Master and Past Provincial Grand Master of Ayrshire.*

19

5. He had an empathy with masonry. Hans Hecht got it right when he averred that Burns was at heart a Freemason "before he saw the light". It could truly be said that he accepted what one might call "the Lessing Concept" – the basic concept of a brotherhood of man under the fatherhood of God.

6. He found that the fundamental truths which Freemasonry has embodied in its philosophy, its thinking and its ideals were precisely the same as the dynamic principles and humanitarian aims and ideals which permeated his whole being. Hence throughout the whole range of his writings, letters, songs and poems we find innumerable examples of those basic truths which Freemasons recognise as flowing from the fountain-head of Masonic philosophy and teaching.

> "Many and sharp the numerous ills
> Inwoven with our frame!
> More pointed still we make ourselves
> Regret, remorse and shame!
> And Man, whose heaven-erected face
> The smiles of love adorn –
> Man's inhumanity to man
> Makes countless thousands mourn!"

Take the letter – one of our priceless possessions – sent to his brethren from Edinburgh; the letter in which he pleads for a sympathetic understanding and treatment of Lodge debtors "craving days", beginning with the salutation:

> "Men and Brethren,
> I am truly sorry . . ."

Generally we concern ourselves with the sentiments expressed in the letter. I believe we should look anew at the salutation:

> "Men and Brethren"

I believe that this is more than a courteous greeting; I believe that in this phrase Burns is recognising that Masons are human (men), creatures of their time, subject to all the pressures, all the vagaries, all the constraints of life, but as Brethren they have obligations, that in their relations with their fellows they must be motivated and controlled by a spirit of true brotherhood.

Burns in this phase underlines the Mason's obligation as a citizen.

In the Farewell to his own Brethren does he not take the concept a stage further and spell out the guide lines for community living?

> "May Freedom, harmony and love
> Unite you in the grand design
> Beneath th' Omniscient eye above
> The Glorious Architect Divine
> That you may keep th' unerring line
> Still rising by the plummet's law
> Till Order bright completely Shine
> Shall be my pray'r when far awa'."

20

and do we not see a further extension of the concept in the oft repeated lines:-

> "Then let us pray that come it may,
> As come it will for a' that,"

Many and varied have been the illogical and nonsensical interpretations of this stanza. Does the stanza not simply portray for us a vision, an expression of a world citizenship, a world where, in our relations with others, we are actuated by feelings of true fraternalism, tolerance, understanding, compassion?

Let me end on a note of repetition:-

Burns found Masonry a moving and stimulating experience.

I believe Burns found in Masonry something akin to his native genius.

He was a dedicated Freemason.

He found pleasure and profit in this association with his fellows and in return he has given us equal pleasure and profit.

He delighted in the Craft and in this respect he is a worthy example to us all.

Indeed only a lover of the Craft could have written so freely and so uninhibitedly of the badge we are all so proud to wear: The Master's Apron.

> "Ther's many a badge that's unco braw
> Wi' ribbon, lace, and tape on;
> Let kings and princes wear them a'
> Gie me the Master's Apron, etc."

Chapter Four

ROBERT BURNS – FREEMASON

(By Fred J. Belford, MA, FEIS, Lodge No. 1029, Hon. Member Lodge No. 135.)

Among the great men whose memories Scotsmen in particular have been delighted to perpetuate few, if any, have been held in greater love and admiration than Robert Burns, the national poet of Scotland. Indeed, the enthusiasm which is aroused as each succeeding January comes round is a source of continual wonder to other nations and it certainly has no parallel in any other country. In this article we shall deal mainly with Burns' activities as a Freemason and as such Scotsmen should be immensely proud that the Bard was a member of the Fraternity. As we shall see Masonry and Scottish Masonry, at that, played no mean part in giving to the world the poetry of Robert Burns.

According to Dr Halliday, "One prime factor which assisted to unite all classes in eighteenth-century Scotland into a recognised brotherhood, and provided the opportunity and sanction for voluntary co-operation, was the bond of Freemasonry; not Freemasonry as we know it today with all its modern trappings and symbolic teaching, but the earlier jolly Brotherhood with its gatherings at the local inn. There is no cause for wonder or surprise that in the fullness of time Robert Burns became a Freemason: the wonder would have been if he had not." The heart of the poet was a soil ideal to the seeds of Freemasonry, for the beautiful teaching of the Craft is alive with the very essence of poetry. His abiding interest in, and love of, all that was in any way connected with the Order no doubt coloured much of his poetry and ultimately found expression in "A man's a man for a' that," the great poem on the Brotherhood of Man. In that poem, and especially in the last verse, we find expressed the whole of the grand ideal of freemasonry. This is not to say, however, that such a poem was wholly inspired by Freemasonry, because Burns would have written in this vein had he never entered the door of a Masonic Lodge.

Masonry made a direct appeal to one of his temperament, loving as he did social companions, and who himself was the life and soul in any congenial company. Not only so, but Freemasonry was flourishing so strongly in Tarbolton at the time that it was to be expected that in due course he would enter fervently into everything concerned with the Order. Freemasonry gave him an impetus, and we cannot doubt that the hours he spent with the Brethren helped in no small way to lighten many a dark hour in his life and cheered him between his periods of despondency.

> "The social, friendly, honest man
>   Whate'er he be,
> 'Tis he fulfils great Nature's plan
>   And none but he."

Another typically Masonic verse by him is:
> "A' ye whom social pleasure charms,
> Whose heart the tide of kindness warms,
> Wha hold your being on the terms

'Each aid the others,'
Come to my bowl, come to my arms,
My friends, my brothers."

His enthusiasm for Freemasonry was mainly attributable to his sociable dispo-
sition, and there is sufficient testimony that Burns was not given to conviviality
merely to satisfy a craving for strong drink. But the influence of Masonry on his
life must be put into its proper perspective, for there is no denying that the part it
played in the publication of his poems cannot be overlooked. It would appear to be
manifestly unfair on the part of Carlyle and several others of his biographers that
either not a word has come from their pen or, if it did, it was to depreciate his connection with the Craft. In fact, to omit or slight Burns' Masonic career is surely
unjust to him and to Freemasonry. His association with the Brethren indeed was a
means of enabling him to meet persons of a higher social status than himself and of
introducing him to families of distinction, especially during his stay in Edinburgh,
and at the same time helping to raise him from obscurity to the place he so richly
deserved – the national poet of Scotland.

During the fifteen years (1781-1796) which covered his Masonic career he
devoted himself wholeheartedly to all that pertained to the Brotherhood, making
that "daily advancement" of which our First Charge stresses the importance.

Burns' Masonic life might conveniently be divided, like all Gaul, into three
parts. The first part includes his initiation into the Fraternity and his active work in
his native county of Ayr, the historic home of Freemasonry. Included also in this
period is the publication of the now famous and priceless Kilmarnock Edition of
his poems. The second comprises the two periods he spent in Edinburgh, where
Masonry did not enter particularly prominently into his life[1], probably because of
the assiduous attention he was giving to the publication of his Edinburgh Edition.
The chief matter of interest in his visit to the Capital is the controversy surround-
ing his supposed inauguration as Poet Laureate of Lodge Canongate Kilwinning.
The third division concerns his declining years in Dumfriesshire, where he again
resumed his Masonic interests though, partly owing to illness, to a lesser extent.

In 1781 the Burns family tenanted the farm of Lochlea, near Tarbolton, having
come there from Mount Oliphant in 1777. Robert, before joining the Craft, had
attended a school in Kirkoswald in the practical use of instruments concerned with
mensuration and surveying, the Square, the Level, etc., and so, at the beginning of
his Masonic career he was already well versed in the operative uses of a mason's
working tools. He tells us that while in Kirkoswald he went on with a high hand at
his geometry until the sun entered Virgo, which was always a carnival in his
bosom.

The history of Freemasonry round about the period with which we are dealing
was of a somewhat turbulent nature. On 17 May 1771 Lodge Tarbolton Kilwinning
had received its Charter from Mother Kilwinning. Twenty of the Brethren, seeing
clearly that the power of the latter was on the decline, wished to erect a Lodge
under the jurisdiction of the Grand Lodge of Scotland which since 1736 was
steadily growing in power[2] and so St David, Tarbolton, No 174, was chartered on
5 February 1773. Those who were left in the original Lodge Tarbolton Kilwinning
also saw the wisdom of working under Grand Lodge and so they too applied for
recognition. This resulted in 1774 in the erection of a new Lodge, St James,

23

Tarbolton, No 178. The Grand Master Mason at the time was John, 3rd Duke of Athole. No doubt a little jealousy in this case crept in over the original secession. At the same time the Brethren were fully aware that there was not room in such a small village as Tarbolton for two Lodges. It was accordingly agreed to sink all differences and the two Lodges combined on 25 June 1781, under the name of Lodge St David, Tarbolton, since this Lodge held "the oldest charter" from Grand Lodge, "probably a compliment or concession," according to Chambers, "designed to appease the schismatic body".

Into this united Lodge Burns, nine days after the union, was initiated in his twenty-third year, and his name recorded in the Minute Book as follows: – "Sederunt for 4 July. Robert Burns in Lockly was entered an Apprentice, Joph. Norman M.." His initiation fee was 12s. 6d., and was paid on the same day.

The Lodge met in John Richard's public house where the Bachelors' Club founded in 1780 by Burns and other kindred spirits, had a room. This house has been recently renovated and is now in an excellent state of repair. The following is from the preamble which Burns himself wrote regarding this club:

> "Of birth or blood we do not boast,
> Nor gentry does our club afford;
> But ploughmen and mechanics we
> In nature's simple dress record." [3]

The social urge and the opportunities he had for expressing his thoughts fluently there were very soon to bear fruit in his Lodge.

Shortly after his initiation he removed to Irvine to learn flax-dressing. This upset for a time his Masonic attendances, but on 1 October 1781, he was passed to the Fellowcraft Degree and raised to the Degree of Master as set forth in the brief Minute:[4] "Robert Burns in Lochly was passed and raised," signed by the Master, the Wardens, Secretary and Treasurer.

The united Lodge enjoyed a brief history of only a few months,[5] but a history rendered glorious for all time by having the peculiar distinction of making Burns a Freemason. Nor did the union appear to have been a happy one. Apparently that harmony which should characterise Masons the world over was lacking. At any rate, a fresh disruption took place the following year, June 1782. Burns was one of the seceders. Some of the members doubtless objected to Lodge St James losing its identity and it was to be expected that it was only a matter of time before a separate Lodge would be formed. This materialised on 17 June 1782, under its former name of St James, Tarbolton. Some years later, a list of its members was sent to Grand Lodge, and the names of these members are found engrossed in the books there. Burns' name does not appear in this list, possibly because only the names of entrants, after the Lodge had become a separate body, were submitted to Grand Lodge. This is borne out by the fact that the name of Gilbert Burns, who was made a Mason five years after the erection of Lodge St James, appears only about a dozen names from the top. On the other hand, this neglect may have been occasioned by the carelessness of Grand Lodge officials at the time who have been alleged to have been very much averse to such dry labour as the enrolment of names. Lodge Tarbolton Kilwinning St James now appears on the Roll of the

Grand Lodge of Scotland at No. 135 and possesses a large commodious hall of its own in the centre of the village. Lodge St David became dormant in 1843, but was reopened in 1869 as No. 133, with Mauchline as its meeting place. It has some interesting relics[6] consisting of jewels, plate for printing Diplomas of the Lodge, Master's chair, chest, Lodge glasses, toddy-ladles, and a Minute Book. These are now believed to be in safe custody in Ayr.

At a meeting of the Grand Lodge of Scotland in May 1951, it was reported that the Minute Books containing details of the initiation of Burns into Freemasonry, now in private hands, were valued at £3,000. The Grand Librarian informed the Grand Committee that a lady in Kilmarnock had in her possession certain old Minute Books and other items lately belonging to Lodge St David, No. 133. When the Lodge became dormant in 1843 the Charter was recovered by the Provincial Grand Master and returned to Grand Lodge.[7] The Minute Books passed into private hands. The Lodge was reponed in 1869 and, although the Charter was returned, the Minute Books were not. In 1925 the law agent advised the Grand Committee that an action would have to be raised against the lady if it were decided to prove title. No action was taken.

Burns's name is not recorded in the Minutes of Lodge St James until 1784. But his keen interest in the Lodge is evident from the following letter in his handwriting, but not necessarily composed by him, addressed to the Master, Sir John Whiteford, Bart, of Ballochmyle, on behalf of the seceders in connection with the dispute, towards the end of 1782:

"Sir, – We who subscribe to this are members of St James's Lodge, Tarbolton, and one of us in the office of Warden, and as we have the honour of having you for Master of our Lodge, we hope you will excuse this freedom, as you are the proper person to whom we ought to apply. We look on our Mason Lodge to be a serious matter, both with respect to the character of Masonry itself, and likewise as it is a charitable society. This last, indeed, does not interest you farther than a benevolent heart is interested in the welfare of its fellow creatures; but to us, Sir, who are of the lower orders of mankind, to have a fund in view, on which we may with certainty depend to be kept from want should we be in circumstances of distress, or old age, that is a matter of high importance.

We are sorry to observe that our Lodge's affairs, with respect to its finances, have for a good while been in a wretched condition. We have considerable sums in bills which lie by without being paid, or put in execution, and many of our members never mind their yearly dues, or anything else belonging to our Lodge. And since the separation from St David's we are not even sure of our existence as a Lodge. There has been a dispute before the Grand Lodge, but how decided, or if decided at all, we know not.

For these and other reasons we humbly beg the favour of you, as soon as convenient, to call a meeting, and let us consider on some means to retrieve our wretched affairs.

We are, etc."

On 30 June 1784 the famous Manson's Inn, the Cross Keys,[8] became the meeting place, the proprietor being Treasurer to the Lodge. This old inn is no longer in existence, but its locus has been indicated by a tablet placed in a corner of the garden. A month later, on 27 July, Burns was elected Depute Master, an office which was then elective and of much more practical importance than it is today. This position carried with it the active duties of a Master, who in these days was little more than a figurehead, and attended meetings but rarely. So Burns was in reality the virtual head of the Lodge, and it is on record that he carried through his work with marked ability. He held the Depute Mastership till St John's Day, 1788.

"Oft have I met your social band,
And spent the cheerful festive night;
Oft honour'd with supreme command
Presided o'er the Sons of Light."

His first Minute as Depute Master, and which is wholly in his handwriting, although unsigned, shows his keen interest in the Lodge:

"This night the Lodge met and ordered four pounds of candles and one quire of eight-pence paper for the use of the Lodge, which money was laid out by the Treasurer and the candles and paper laid in accordingly."

By his enthusiasm he justified his election to the leading place in the Lodge. Robert Chambers tells us "that according to the reports of old associates he was so keen a Mason that he would hold Lodges for the admission of new members in his own house."[9] and it was at one of these that his brother Gilbert was admitted to the Craft.

He was himself most faithful in his attendance at Lodge meetings. During 1785 he was present at nine meetings, and it was because of an incident at one of these where the "vainglorious tendencies" of the village schoolmaster gave birth to his amusing poem, "Death and Doctor Hornbook". The story is so well known that there is no need to detail it here. The famous colloquy between himself and Death has been read by thousands with amusement and delight and has conferred an immortality on John Wilson, the dominie, which he scarcely deserved.[10]

A quaint regulation, dated 7 December 1785, written by John Wilson (Dr Hornbook) and signed "Robert Burness" is worthy of mention at this point.

"The Lodge thought proper to writing that old regulation. That who ever stands as Master shall be bound at the entry of a new member for that member's dues if the money is not paid or security such as the Lodge shall approve of."

In 1786 Burns again attended nine meetings, at the second of which, on 1 March, he initiated, passed and raised his brother Gilbert. It is interesting to note that he signed the Minute of this meeting "Robert Burns." Up to this date he had used the signature "Robert Burness." Apparently during all this time, though living some miles from the village, he never missed a single meeting of his Lodge and on several occasions, as we have seen, he held subordinate meetings in Mauchline, thus doing his utmost to promote the tenets of Freemasonry.

For a time at least Gilbert Burns took an active part in the affairs of the Lodge. His name appears in the Minute Book on five separate occasions between 11 December 1786 and 21 December 1787, and he occupied the Chair on two occasions, when the Lodge met at Mauchline on 18 and 20 November 1788. In July 1787 he had a loan from the Lodge of £6 5s. (a not uncommon practice in those days), which he repaid in June 1788.

It soon became apparent that the Brethren were not satisfied with their meeting place in Manson's Tavern, and they began to look around for more suitable quarters. We find a curious proposition recorded in the Minute of 15 June:

"It was proposed by the Lodge that, as they much wanted a Lodge-room, a proposal be laid before the heritors, who are intending to build a steeple here, that the Lodge will contribute to the building of a Lodge-room, as the basis of that steeple; and that, from the funds of the Lodge, they offer fifteen pounds, besides what will be advanced from the particular friends of the Lodge. In order that this proposal be properly laid before the heritors, five persons, namely the Right Worshipful Master, Brother McMath, Brother Burns, Brother Wodrow, Brother William Andrew – are appointed to meet on Saturday at one o'clock, to draw up a proposal to lay before the heritors on Friday first."

What became of the proposal is unknown[11]. There is no record of the Lodge ever having assembled in the base of the proposed steeple.

In all Burns signed twenty-nine Minutes as Depute Master, and three are wholly his penmanship. He also subscribed his initials to a postscript. One of these signatures was stolen and never recovered. A second attempt was made to steal another part of the precious volume, but the theft was discovered in time and the stolen portion returned. It can be seen neatly pasted in its original setting. This Minute Book is, of course, of especial interest and is fully preserved in the Lodge which also treasures the Master's chair, footstool, apron and the mallet used by him when presiding at its meetings, the candlesticks and other articles associated with him during his term of office. Also to be seen is an old Tyler's sword. The Lodge Bible[12], which bears the date 1775, was one of the poet's possessions and was presented to the Lodge by his brother Gilbert and himself. It was purchased by the Lodge on 29 July 1786. The Minute reads – "Bible cost 13s., lettering (i.e., the printed name of the Lodge outside) cost 3s." The Lodge has also the oft-quoted letter addressed by him from Edinburgh to his Lodge Brethren, prior to his Highland tour, intimating the reason for his inability to be present at one of their important meetings.

At this point it might be interesting and enlightening to enumerate some of the Rules applicable to Lodge St James in Burns' day:

"At the third stroke of the Grand Master's hammer silence shall be maintained under a penalty of twopence.
"Whosoever shall break a drinking glass at any meeting shall be liable to the instant payment of sixpence sterling for it, and the same sum for every other he may break before he leaves the room or company.
"Those not at meetings within an hour of the fixed time shall be fined twopence.
"If any Brother be so unfortunate as to have disordered his senses by strong liquors and thereby rendered himself incapable of behaving himself decently, peaceably and kind towards those around him, such Brother coming to the Lodge in that condition to the disturbance and disgust of his Brethren, shall be prudently ordered away to some place of safety in the meantime, and at the next meeting shall submit to such censure and admonition from the Chair, and to such a fine inflicted by the Lodge on him as to them may appear proper to his crime, and deter him from it in all time coming.
"Whereas a Lodge always means a company of worthy men and circumspect, gathered together in order to promote charity, friendship, civility and good neighbourhood, it is enacted that no member of this Lodge shall speak slightingly, detractingly or calumniously of any of his Brethren behind their backs, so as to damage them in their professions or reputations without any certain grounds, and any member committing any such offence must humble himself by asking on his knees the pardon of such person or persons as his folly or malice hath aggrieved. Obstinate refusal to comply with this rule of the Brethren assembled shall be met with expulsion from the Lodge with every mark of ignominy and disgrace that is consistent with Justice and Freemasonry."

The excellent manner in which Burns carried out his duties may be gauged not only from his attendance record and his care of the Minutes of Proceedings, but also from the following letter written by Professor Dugald Stewart:

"In Summer 1787 I passed some weeks in Ayrshire, and saw Burns occasionally . . . I was led by curiousity to attend for an hour or two a Masonic Lodge in Mauchline, where Burns presided. He had occasion to make some short unpremeditated compliments to different individuals from whom he had no occasion to expect a visit, and everything he said was happily conceived and forcibly as well as fluently expressed. His manner of speaking in public had evidently the marks of some practice in extempore elocution.

Professor Dugald Stewart, who was then resident in Catrine, was admitted an honorary member of Lodge St James, and the Minute recording his admission was signed "Robert Burns, D.M." The Professor was a member of Lodge Canongate Kilwinning and proved himself a very good friend to the poet during his residence in Edinburgh and according to Burns was "the most perfect character I ever saw." Their early morning walks on the Braid Hills were greatly enjoyed by both.

During Burns' term of office as Depute Master the Brethren were convened no fewer than seventy times, at thirty-three of which he was present, and his attendances would doubtless have been more numerous had he not been away from the district for lengthy periods in these two momentous years, 1787-1788.

It is generally believed that he visited a number of Lodges in his immediate vicinity. At a meeting, on 27 March 1786, of Lodge Loudoun Kilwinning Newmilns, of which his friend Gavin Hamilton was Master, he was introduced to the Brethren and "much to the satisfaction of the Lodge", was admitted a member, Brother John Morton being "answerable for" his "admission money".

A writer in the *Burns Chronicle* of 1893 states that the poet was present at a Mason Lodge held at Sorn on 5 October 1786, and in the same Annual for 1905 we have it that he "mixed with the Brethren of the Craft in Lodge St Andrew at Irvine,"[13] and that "it is conjectured that it was in that town" that the "stanza added in a Mason Lodge" was tacked on to his bacchanalian song, whose refrain is the "big-bellied bottle":

> "Then fill up a bumper, and make it o'erflow,
> And honours Masonic prepare for to throw;
> May every true Brother of the Compass and Square
> Have a big-bellied bottle when harass'd with care!"

Notwithstanding the long distance he had to travel he never found the road to and from the Lodge wearisome. The thought of the meeting ahead and poetical composition so intruded into his mind that the miles would seem shorter. Masonic thoughts which are easily detectable in his poems can no doubt be traced to these evening walks. It has been said that Burns' attendances at Masonic meetings led him into excesses. His brother Gilbert's testimony on this point is surely an effective answer to those who would cast this slur on the poet:

"Towards the end of the period under review (in his twenty-fourth year), and soon after his father's death, he was furnished with the subject of his epistle to John Rankin. During this period, also, he became a Freemason, which was his first introduction to the life of a boon companion. Yet, notwithstanding these circumstances, and the praise he has bestowed on Scotch Drink (which seems to have misled his historians) I do not recollect

28

during these seven years, nor till towards the end of his commencing author (when his growing celebrity occasioned his often being in company), to have ever seen him intoxicated; nor was he at all given to drinking."

By this time Burns had become recognised as an outstanding poet, and his poems had been well received by those who heard them. It was during the winter of 1785-1786 that the full strength of his genius shone forth as at no other time. His poems were known to comparatively few, however, but among those few were the members of his own Lodge, and they from the first recognised the poet's merits. On the suggestion of Gavin Hamilton, a lawyer, and landlord of Mossgiel Farm, Burns was persuaded to collect his writings and publish them by subscription, and so early in 1786 he went to Kilmarnock to arrange for this being done. He took up the suggestion with enthusiasm, and it is not too much to say that the Brethren of his Lodge were, out of friendship to their brother Mason, largely responsible for the first edition of poems. The Brethren of Lodge St John Kilwinning, Kilmarnock, which he frequently visited, also assisted very handsomely by subscribing freely themselves and getting others to supplement their action. They agreed to take 350 copies as soon as they were printed, the Right Worshipful Master subscribing for 35 copies and another Brother for 75. This volume might with every justification be called a Masonic Edition. Burns himself could not find the means to publish it, but his Masonic Brethren loyally supported him in ensuring the success of the venture, which was, as might be expected, dedicated to Gavin Hamilton. John Wilson, an enthusiastic Mason, was the printer of this First Edition. It cannot fail to be noticed that contact with Freemasons and Freemasonry runs like a golden thread throughout the poet's life, and the friends he met in the Craft had no small share in shaping his destiny. Well may Scottish Masons claim to have "deserved well of humanity," for they saved from oblivion these gems of poetry and song which came from "the soul of a man".

Meantime he was having serious domestic troubles, Jean Armour and Mary Campbell had entered into his life, and his farming losses were heavy. The Highland Mary episode wherein Mary Campbell and Robert Burns enacted their betrothal, on opposite banks of the River Ayr, with ritualistic ceremony had a Masonic touch about it: vows of fidelity were pronounced, Bibles exchanged, the names of the contracting parties being written on the fly-leaves, along with Burns Masonic Mark with, on the one leaf, "And ye shall not swear by my name falsely. . . . I am the Lord" from Leviticus, Chap. XIX, v. 12, and on the other, "Thou shall not forswear thyself, but shalt perform unto the Lord thine oaths" from St Matthew, Chap. V., v. 33. This historic Bible with the signatures erased and part of the "Mark" obliterated fell into the hands of a relative of Mary Campbell after her death, was purchased in Canada for £25, and may be seen in the Burns Museum in the Monument on the banks of the Doon.

Burns was so weighed down by despondency that it was in the hope of bettering his position that he made up his mind on 12 June to proceed to Jamaica to take up an appointment there. One can easily understand in what stress he must have been when he entertained such a thought. Freemasonry had taught him "ever to remember that the Almighty had implanted in his breast a sacred attachment towards that country whence he derived his birth and infant nurture". In his early years he had again and again nourished the hope that he would "for puir auld Scotland's sake" make "some usefu' plan or book" or "sing a sang at least".

He was re-elected to the Depute Mastership on 16 June 1786, his brother Gilbert going into the Senior Warden's Chair. It is rather curious that he should have allowed his name to go forward on that date for re-election to this office as he had already set his mind on Jamaica, and on 23 June he recited his "Farewell to the Brethren of St James's Lodge". This meeting was probably that to which he had sent his poetical invitation to his doctor, Dr Mackenzie of Mauchline.

> "Friday first's the day appointed
> By our Right Worshipful anointed,
>   To hold our grand procession;
>   To get a blad o' Johnny's morals,
> And taste a swatch o' Manson's barrels
>   I' the way of our profession.
> "Our Master and the Brotherhood
>   Would a' be glad to see you;
> For me I would be mair than proud
>   To share the mercies wi' you.
> If Death, then, wi' skaith, then,
>   Some mortal heart is hechtin',
> Inform him, and storm him,
>   That Saturday you'll fecht him."

The "Day appointed" was the anniversary of St John the Baptist, and this was observed by the Brethren walking in procession. It was "Carnival day in Tarbolton". As Mid-summer Day was one of the few occasions on which Freemasonry came before the public, Burns was especially anxious that there should be a good muster of the Brethren and so used to address the members personally. The poem quoted above has been preserved with the signature "Robert Burns, D.M." and dated from "Mossgiel, 14 June, A.M. 1790".

The famous Kilmarnock Edition of his poems was published on 31 July, met with instant success, and he suddenly leapt into fame. The whole 600 copies were bought up in the matter of a few weeks, he himself being richer by £20. What these volumes are worth today it would be difficult to assess.

His passage to Jamaica had been booked. His vessel was due to sail at the end of November. He had written his "Farewell to the Brethren", and Scotland seemed on the point of losing her illustrious son, when a letter written by Doctor Blacklock to a friend[14], and which Burns received, caused him to change his mind, overthrow all his schemes, and remain in his native land, where new prospects to his poetic ambition were opened up. To quote his own words:

> "I had just taken the last farewell of a few friends; my chest was on the road to Greenock; I had composed the last song I should ever measure in Caledonia; when Dr Blacklock's opinion that I would meet with encouragement in Edinburgh for a second edition fired me so much that I posted away to that city."

This "last song" was "The gloomy night is gathering fast". Had Burns's intention to emigrate been fulfilled it is more than likely that his great "Farewell" poem would have concluded his active connection with Scottish Freemasonry.

"Adieu! a heart-warm, fond adieu
    Dear brothers of the mystic tie!
Ye favour'd, yet enlighten'd few,
    Companions of my social joy!
Tho' I to foreign lands must hie,
    Pursuing Fortune's slidd'ry ba',
With melting heart, and brimful eye.
    I'll mind you still, tho' far awa'.

Oft have I met your social band,
    And spent the cheerful festive night;
Oft honour'd with supreme command,
    Presided o'er the sons of light;
Any by that hieroglyphic bright,
    Which none but craftsmen ever saw!
Strong mem'ry on my heart shall write
    Those happy scenes when far awa'.

May freedom, harmony and love,
    Unite you in the grand design,
Beneath th'omniscient eye above,
    The glorious architect divine!
That you may keep th'unerring line,
    Still rising by the plummet's law,
Till order bright completely shine,
    Shall be my prayer when far awa'.

And you, farewell! whose merits claim,
    Justly that highest badge to wear!
Heav'n bless your honour'd, noble name,
    To masonry and Scotia dear!
A last request, permit me here,
    When yearly ye assemble a',
One round, I ask it with a tear,
    To him, the bard that's far awa'!"

Some of his biographers have stated that by the time he reached the last stanza many of the Brethren were in tears.

The person entitled to wear the "Highest Badge" was the Master of the Lodge, and the Master of St James at that date was Captain, afterwards Major-General James Montgomerie, a younger brother of Colonel Hugh Montgomerie, afterwards Earl of Eglinton. Some authorities assert that the reference is to the Grand Master Mason of Scotland, William Wallace, Sheriff of Ayr. The poet's request to be remembered yearly at the festive board is regularly honoured in Lodge St James.

On 26 October Burns was made an honorary member of Kilmarnock Kilwinning St John, No. 24 (now No. 22), which met in the old Commercial Inn, now demolished, in Croft Street. He was pleased at the honour conferred upon him and in recognition wrote the stanzas beginning "Ye sons of Old Killie, assembled by Willie", the Christian name of the reigning Master whose name appears at the close of the following Minute:

"Oct. 26th, 1786."

"Present the Right Worshipful Master, Deputy Master and several Brethren, when John Galt, farmer, in Cressland, was, upon his petition, made and entered Apprentice. At same time Robert Burns, poet, Mauchline, a member of St James's Tarbolton, was made an honorary member of this Lodge."

(Signed) "WILL PARKER."

EDITOR'S FOOTNOTES TO CHAPTER FOUR

1. The second and third parts of this Life are detailed in the appropriate sections of this work.
2. This opinion is not shared by the Editor, whose view is reflected in Chapter One and which is supported by documentary evidence.
3. This was not written by Burns but by his friend and "Brither Poet", David Sillar.
4. For the complete Minute read the account in Chapter One.
5. Until 5 December 1781.
6. These relics are the possession of Lodge St James and are still to be seen in the Lodge.
7. The Editor does not share this view; a full account is to be found in Chapter Two.
8. Manson's Inn and the Cross Keys were separate establishments. Lodge St James was re-formed in the Cross Keys and moved to Manson's Inn in 1784.
9. There is no documentary proof for such a statement. Furthermore, as stated in the Minute, Brother Gilbert Burns was admitted to the Craft at a meeting in Mauchline of Lodge St James.
10. ". . ., which he scarcely deserved." is, in the Editor's view, a harsh and unfair comment.
11. The proposal was abandoned. Manson obtained the adjoining property and the Lodge remained there for some time.
12. The Bible was purchased by Burns for the Lodge. Details of the cost etc., are to be found in the Treasurer's Book, not the Minute Book.
13. The Editor can find no documentary proof that Burns ever attended Lodge St Andrew, Irvine.
14. The friend was Rev Dr Lawrie, Loudoun, who had sent a copy of Burns' poems to him.

Chapter 5

THE IMMORTAL MEMORY OF ROBERT BURNS

Toast proposed at the Burns Night
of Lodge St Vincent, Sandyford, No. 553
by Dr R. T. Halliday, JP,
Junior Grand Warden, Grand Lodge of Scotland

Scotland today is a vastly different conception from the Scotland of the close of the eighteenth century. For this change, which is commonly called Progress, many factors might be deemed responsible, each in its own measure; but outstanding among them is the transformation of the industrial system from handicraft to machine production. When the subject of our theme was ushered into a world of sorrows on that memorable 25th January 1759, the social status of the Scots toiler was pronouncedly individualistic. In a sense quite unknown in these modern days each man was his own master, using his own brain and employing his own tools and implements, and bargaining with a merchant without restriction or any outside interference for the disposal of the products of his energies. He depended very largely upon himself. If he owed allegiance to anything it was to the kirk, which was peculiarly powerful in its narrow piety among the Scottish peasantry. But in his secular life he endeavoured to maintain a sturdy independence with all its privileges and all its responsibilities. Sometimes he succeeded and sometimes he did not. Robert Burns as a humble tiller of the soil was in the latter category: his misfortune, but certainly not his fault.

Man, however, particularly of the Burns temperament – full of buoyant, jovial and passionate humanity – cannot be independent in a social sense and yet be happy. Social intercourse is as much a necessity for him as food and raiment, and what the literary salons of Glasgow and Edinburgh were to the city dwellers of these early days, the rockins and kirns were to the Ayrshire peasants. One prime factor which assisted to unite all classes in eighteenth century Scotland into a recognised brotherhood, and provided the opportunity and sanction for voluntary co-operation, was the bond of Freemasonry; not Freemasonry as we know it today with all its modern trappings and symbolic teaching, but the earlier jolly brotherhood with its gatherings in the local inn. There is no cause for wonder or surprise that in the fullness of time Robert Burns became a Freemason; the wonder would have been if he had not.

It is not my intention to deal with the poet's youth and its hardships which, while stimulating his muse, laid the foundation for his life-long infirmity; nor his poetic flights in love and sympathy, in wit and satire, in reverence and tribulation; nor his admitted frailties which drew upon him the severity of the kirk and of the sanctimonious – whom he dubbed the "unco guid" – and for which he in fullest measure tholed his assize. Each of those aspects in the life of Burns has been written of, debated upon, and criticised a multitude of times; often with the muckrake by those with but hazy understanding of his times and circumstances, and conveniently unmindful of the record of the sweet singer of Israel or the founder of the Holy Temple as given in our Volume of the Sacred Law, compared with either of whom Robert Burns was a very saint in morality. I am not out to offer apologies for faults or excuses for failings. I only claim for Burns a square deal, which has been woefully lacking with some so-called friends and biographers. But what most appropriately concerns us in this place and at this time is his close association with, and enthusiasm for, our Masonic ideal, the Brotherhood of Man; and the steps in his Masonic career are by no means the least significant or inspiring in his brief but chequered life. Let me in summarised fashion in the limited time at my disposal refer to these under the following heads:

1. His entry into the Craft at Tarbolton.
2. His revolt with his confrères against presumed injustice.
3. His keen interest in the Craft and its effects
4. The End of the Road.

We can assuredly find in each phase something notable to engage our thoughts and if possible enhance our esteem.

The Burns family removed from Mount Oliphant, near Alloway, to the farm of Lochlea, near Mauchline, in 1777[1]; and in the following year Robert, then at the close of his teens but the chief labourer on the farm, was sent to Kirkoswald to imbibe the rudiments of mensuration and dialling. His regular work and those additional studies made him familiar with the operative uses of the essential tools of a mason, the Rule and Line, the Level and the Square. This operative foundation in such a nature aroused we know the speculative fancy, for on his return to Lochlea he founded with some boon companions the famed Bachelors' Club, a small but select literary society which included David Sillar and John Wilson[2], the immortal "Dr Hornbook". Scotland at this time was comparatively well supplied with Masonic lodges. Edinburgh boasted sixteen, all in flourishing condition; while Dumfries, with but 8,000 inhabitants, had no less than five. Tarbolton, the nearest village centre, had two lodges – St David, No. 174, and St James, No. 178 – which united in June 1781, under the name St David, that lodge "having the oldest charter" from Grand Lodge, although not the older lodge of the twain. Nine days after this fateful union – to wit, on 4 July 1781 – Robert Burns was initiated. He was sponsored by Alexander Wood[3], a tailor, and the entry in the minute book, which is still extant and carefully preserved[4], although unfortunately not in the custody of those to whom it legally, morally and masonically belongs, reads: "Sederant for 4th July, Robt. Burns in Lochly was entered an apprentice. Joph. Norman, M." The volume at present forms an attraction in a village hostelry.

The Lodge met in John Richard's public-house, where the Bachelors' Club had a room, and from this time onward we may safely say that Burns was an ardent Freemason. The principles which were then inculcated made a direct appeal to his nature, and they remained with him to the end. Shortly after his initiation Burns left the district for Irvine, to train for a flax-dressing experiment which proved a failure. His[5] heckling shop caught fire and his partner swindled him. But while still at Irvine he travelled to Tarbolton on 1 October 1781, to attend the Lodge, and the minute of that date records that he was passed and raised, Henry Cowan being Master. His association with Irvine was renewed some years later under presumably happier circumstances, and on visiting[6] Lodge St Andrew there he is said to have composed the stanza of his bacchanalian song:

"Then fill up a bumper and make it o'erflow,
And honours Masonic prepare for to throw:
May ev'ry true Brother of the Compass and Square
Have a big-belly'd bottle when harass'd with care!"

By that time he well knew what care meant.

It is unnecessary to recapitulate here the oft-told tale of the historic split in the united Lodge St David, the raiding of the charter chest (in the custody of Richard) for the recovery of the Lodge St James charter, and the subsequent proceedings in the Sheriff Court at Ayr. In none of these was Burns directly involved. The union had never been a happy one, and we find Burns in this second phase among the seceders who successfully re-established Lodge St James, which had originally a Kilwinning warrant. His name is not given in the minutes until nearly two years later. But his keen interest is evident from the letter in his hand-writing addressed to the Master on behalf of the seceders in connection with the dispute. In June, 1784, Lodge St James, having defied the opposition and even the Grand Lodge of Scotland, established itself in the famous Manson's Inn[7], and a month later elected Burns as Depute Master. This position carried with it the active duties of a Master who in those days was but the figurehead. Hence the Bard's lines:

"Of have I met your social band,
And spent the cheerful, festive night;
Oft, honour'd with supreme command,
Presided o'er the Sons of Light."

The first minute, wholly in his handwriting although unsigned is evidence of his interest:

"This night the Lodge met and ordered four pounds of candles and one quire of eight-pence paper for the use of the Lodge, which money was laid out by the Treasurer and the candles and paper laid in accordingly."

He attended nine meetings during 1785 and nine again in 1786, at the second of which – on 1 March – he passed and raised his brother Gilbert[8]. In all he signed 29 minutes as Depute Master, and three are wholly his penmanship. The excellent manner in which he fulfilled his duties may be gauged not only from his attendance record and his care of the minutes of proceedings, but also from the following letter written by Prof Dugald Stewart: "In summer 1787 I passed some weeks in Ayrshire, and saw Burns occasionally . . . I was led by curiosity to attend for an hour or two a Masonic Lodge in Mauchline where Burns presided[9]. He had occasion to make some short unpremeditated compliments to different individuals from whom he had no occasion to expect a visit, and everything he said was happily conceived and forcibly as well as fluently expressed."

It may be interesting and possibly salutary to quote some of the rules of Lodge St James of those days:

"At the third stroke of the Grand Master's hammer silence shall be maintained under a penalty of twopence."

"Whosoever shall break a drinking glass at any meeting shall be liable to the instant payment of sixpence sterling for it, and the same sum for every other he may break before he leaves the room or company."

"Those not at meetings within an hour of the fixed time shall be fined twopence."

"If any brother be so unfortunate as to have disordered his senses by strong liquors and thereby rendered himself incapable of behaving himself decently, peaceably and kind towards those around him, such brother coming to the Lodge in that condition to the disturbance and disgust of his brethren shall be prudently ordered away to some place of safety in the meantime, and at the next meeting shall submit to such censure and admonition from the chair, and to such a fine inflicted by the Lodge on him as to them may appear proper to his crime, and deter him from it in all time coming."

"Whereas a Lodge always means a company of worthy men and circumspect, gathered together in order to promote charity, friendship, civility and good neighbourlyness, it is enacted that no member of this Lodge shall speak slightingly, detractingly or calumniously of any of his brethren behind their backs, so as to damage them in their professions or reputations without any certain grounds, and any member committing such an offence must humble himself by asking on his knees the pardon of such person or persons as his folly or malice hath aggrieved. Obstinate refusal to comply with this rule of the brethren assembled shall be met with expulsion from the Lodge with every mark of ignominy and disgrace that is consistent with Justice and Freemasonry."

It is well to have such regulation and precepts in remembrance when we are regaled with the usual exaggerated reports of the doings of Freemasons in Burns' day.

Had it not been for the brotherhood of Freemasonry in Ayrshire the world today would be immeasurably the poorer. To the appreciation and personal friendship of his Masonic brethren we are indebted for the issue of the first or Kilmarnock edition of the poems of Robert Burns. He was in sore distress of mind when he undertook this, and had just written "The Lament", mourning in lamentation deep "How life and love are all a dream." He went to Kilmarnock to see through the press that now precious volume. While still in residence there he was made an honorary member of Lodge Kilmarnock Kilwinning St John, now No. 22, on 26 October 1786. The Master was Major William Parker, of whom Burns wrote:

> "Ye sons of old Killie, assembled by Willie
>   To follow the noble vocation,
> Your thirfty old mother has scarce such another
>   To sit in that honorèd station."

The song from which this stanza is quoted was said to have been written in the Lodge itself and given by the poet to Major Parker. Brother Parker is said to have subscribed for 35 copies of his forthcoming book; Robert Muir, another of the brethren, disposed of 72 copies; while John Wilson, another brother printed the work. What these Kilmarnock volumes are valued at today is known to most of you. Each is worth its weight in gold; Burns for the whole edition realised but £20.

Freemasonry was again the means of altering and re-shaping his course in life when arrangements had been made for his departure to Jamaica. His friend and brother mason, Dr Blacklock, hinted that a new edition of his poems should be published in Edinburgh and that he should there personally superintend the undertaking. This advice was followed and Burns proceeded to the Metropolis.

EDITOR'S FOOTNOTES TO CHAPTER FIVE

1. In fact, near Tarbolton.
2. Sillar and Wilson were not Founder Members.
3. There is no evidence that Burns was sponsored by Wood. Local tradition has always strongly held to the view that Brother John Rankine, a near farmer-neighbour, was his sponsor.
4. The St David's Minute Books of the period are now with Lodge St James. Read Chapter 3.
5. For "His" read "The".
6. This is pure supposition. There is absolutely no proof that Burns ever attended a Masonic Meeting in Irvine.
7. Lodge St James was re-established in the Cross Keys in 1782 and moved to Manson's Inn in 1784.
8. "He initiated, passed and raised."
9. The Lodge referred to was "St James".

Chapter Six

CALEDONIA'S BARD –
ROBERT BURNS

Lecture by Brother W. Sclater

"We look at our Mason Lodge to be a serious matter." R.B.

During the past 150 years some three thousand books have been written about Scotland's National Poet. The number of speeches and orations is beyond all computation. In face of all this it is difficult to find anything fresh to say. There is however one aspect of the subject which might bear further investigation. The full story of the Poet's association with the Craft has still to be written, and fuller enquiry would undoubtedly bring to light some facts of considerable interest.

Very little light is shed upon the Bard's Masonic life by the numerous biographies which have appeared in the past. The biographers all fight shy of the subject. One gets the impression that there is something resembling a conspiracy of silence on the subject of Freemasonry and what any of them have got to say could pretty well be put on a postcard. This is, perhaps, not altogether surprising. Masons have a habit of shrouding their activities in a veil of secrecy and they cannot complain should the rest of the popular world take little notice of them. The most they can hope for is a passing reference in an obituary notice.

For instance, Dr James Currie of Liverpool, the very first of the official Burns biographers has nothing at all to say about Freemasonry; apparently it was of no interest to him.

Following him came John Gibson Lockhart, whose *Life of the Poet* (1828) was considered to be the last word on the subject and stood as the classical, authoritative biography for many generations. Lockhart was himself a Mason. He was one of that long line of very distinguished men whose names appear on the membership rolls of Canongate Kilwinning No. 2. The most distinguished of all on that list was the name of Brother Robert Burns who, in acknowledgement of his gifts "as a great Poetic Writer" was "assumed a member" on 1 February 1787.

Not only that – Canongate Kilwinning then claimed – and still does claim, albeit on rather slender grounds, that Brother Burns held the office (unconstitutional) of Poet Laureate of the Lodge. In Lockhart's time Lodge Canongate Kilwinning was simply buzzing with Burns' traditions all calling out to be either verified or rejected. What, then, has Lockhart to say on the matter?

> "The Poet was initiated in the mysteries of freemasonry "which was" says his brother "his first introduction to the life of a boon companion." He was introduced to St Mary's Lodge of Tarbolton by John Ranken, a very dissipated man of considerable talents, to whom he afterwards indited a poetical epistle which will be noted in its place."

This is indeed Freemasonry with a small "f". So anxious is Lockhart to get away from an inconvenient topic that he discovers John Ranken as the culprit (without a shred of evidence) and is thus enabled to switch adroitly to another matter which has no connection with Masonry. Lockhart apparently did not carry his researches sufficiently far to enable him to tell the world that the Poet was subsequently passed and raised and a simple query addressed to any knowledgeable member of the craft would have brought to light the fact that there was not, and never had been, a Lodge bearing the name of "St Mary" in Tarbolton. Lordly indifference could not be carried much further!

Coming down nearer to our own time, the 1896 Centenary, we have that very scholarly, that very pungent, penetrating and outspoken study of the *Life, Genius and Achievement of Robert Burns* by W. E. Henley. Henley gives Freemasonry short shrift. He disposes of it in a footnote.

> "Burns was always an enthusiastic Mason. The Masonic idea, whatever that be, went home to him and in honour of the Craft, he wrote some of his poorest verses."

And that's that! Plainly, Henley had no use for Masonry.

These are examples of how the Poet's masonry is handled by biographers. To them, it was a thing of no account. It played no part in the formation of his character or career – contributed nothing to the development of his poetical genius.

That is their implied verdict. It did not apparently occur to them that, to a man who, in the course of ten years, became a member of six different Lodges (not to mention a Royal Arch Chapter), Masonry must surely have had some meaning and influence. We may, with all due deference, dissent from that verdict – we may on examination, come to the conclusions that the verdict is contrary to the evidence – we may, indeed, find ourselves so much at variance with it that we feel emboldened to make the assertion that, but for Freemasonry and Freemasons, Scotland would not have a National Poet, or, at least, that poet would not have been Robert Burns. Let us see then whether we can come to such a conclusion by an examination of the circumstances which led to his being vested with the proud title of "Caledonia's Bard" – the poet of a nation – and how that honour came to be conferred on him as a Brother in the Craft.

The fame of Robert Burns – his reputation as a great poet, as a supreme literary artist, as an outstanding personality – is based on that famous little volume consisting of what the Author in his Preface modestly describes as "trifles composed to amuse himself with the little creations of his own fancy, amid the toil and fatigues of a laborious life" – the volume entitled

POEMS
Chiefly in the Scottish Dialect
by
Robert Burns
Kilmarnock
Printed by JOHN WILSON,
M, D.C.C. LXXXVI.

This is one of the most interesting volumes issued from the press in modern times. It has a particular interest for us as members of the craft by virtue of the inclusion among the "trifles" of a set of verses entitled.

THE FAREWELL
To the Brethren of St James's Lodge, Tarbolton.

39

Now there are few people who could say off-hand where Tarbolton is to be found. It is a little out-of-the-way village in the heart of Ayrshire where the inhabitants pursue the noiseless tenor of their way unnoticed by the bustling world outside. Its chief claim to notice lies in its association with the Author of the Poems. The Tarbolton of 1786 or thereabouts was much less worthy of notice. The Author calls it a "clachan" – a group of dwellings – a hamlet. On a little hill stood the Parish Kirk – bare, gaunt, ugly and round in a clutter of hovels – little one storey cabins built of undressed stones or clay and roofed with straw – so low that a six foot man would have to duck his head to enter[1]. These wretched dwellings were mainly occupied by hand-loom weavers who worked in one apartment and lived in the other. There would be a possible 500 souls including the usual parish tradesmen. We know there was a small cornmill, we know there was a tailor, we know there was one little shop kept by the parish dominie whose scholastic fees did not provide a livelihood. It was a little community practically shut off from the outside world. Nevertheless Tarbolton was not entirely void of cultural activity or social amenity. Although there are no statistics we can assume that there would be the usual dozen or so alehouses in which the Tarboltians could relax.[2] There was nothing unusual about that but they could boast of no less than three poets in and around the clachan. Tarbolton could also boast of a Bachelor's Club, of which our Author was the founder-president, which had regular sessions to debate philosophical problems and engage in other activities not entirely philosophical. Of greater interest to us is the fact that at this period Tarbolton maintained two Masonic lodges.

The first of the Tarbolton lodges was established in 1771, under a Charter of Erection granted by the Auld Mither Ludge of Kilwinning. Mother Kilwinning (now No. 0 on the roll of the Grand Lodge of Scotland) was at this time outside the pale of Grand Lodge. The old lady did not find the gaudy grandeur of that new fangled movement in any way attractive.[3] After all, she had been performing the essential functions of a Grand Lodge from time immemorial – long before Grand Lodges had been invented by ingenious gentlemen masons in London. She had gathered round her skirts some thirty daughters and of these Tarbolton Kilwinning (No. 73) was one. Tarbolton Kilwinning proved to be a sickly child and seems to have had internal trouble from birth. In 1773 disharmony developed to such an extent that many of the Brethren withdrew. They were not, however, to be denied their Masonry and on a petition to Grand Lodge they obtained a charter erecting them as Lodge St David's, No. 174.[4] Not to be outdone, the remnant of Tarbolton Kilwinning, deserting their Auld Mither, petitioned and obtained from Grand Lodge a charter "erecting" them as Lodge St James Tarbolton Kilwinning, No. 178, one of the baits held out by Grand Lodge being that any Kilwinning Lodge accepting its jurisdiction could continue to call itself a Kilwinning Lodge.

For the next seven years in that small community those two lodges sat glowering at each other. In 1781 peace feelers were put out with the result that on 24 June (John the Baptist's Day) the two lodges made a "junction"[5] and on that day they lined up and marched together, as one body in the Grand Annual Procession to the Parish Kirk. They marched under the banner of St David the senior lodge. Ten days later the united lodge held its first regular session and here is the minute of the meeting.

Sederunt for 4th July 1781

ROBERT BURNS in Lochlie was entered an Apprentice.

Signed JO NORMAN, *Master*

On that summer evening Robert Burns, age 23 the young ploughman at Lochlie Farm, had a wash-up, put on his "Sunday sark" and trudged the 4 or 5 miles across the moors to the clachan to be initiated into the mysteries of masonry.[6] Soon after that event, he went down to the seaport town of Irvine to learn the trade of flax-dressing and from Irvine on 1 October, he trudged the 24 miles there and back to Tarbolton to be passed and raised.

The minute recording this is the last reference to Brother Burns in the records of Lodge St David. In the following spring disharmony broke out again and the lodge was rent asunder. The former St James' brethren withdrew and began to reconstitute that lodge. From subsequent events, we know that Brother Burns went with the secessionists, but his name does not appear in the minutes for over two years, nor does he appear in Grand Lodge returns. The only evidence we have is an undated, unaddressed, unsigned draft or copy of a communication on Lodge business in his handwriting. That he was a member during those years and that he had made considerable progress in the science is evidenced by the fact that on 27 July 1784, the brethren of St James' elected him as Depute Master – just three years after his initiation. As Depute Master he ruled and governed the Lodge for two and a half years[7], during which time he attended to the duties of his office with commendable assiduity. During this period his private and personal affairs were not going well – so badly indeed that he decided to leave the country. He obtained a job on a Jamaica sugar plantation and made preparations for his departure. In 1786, on 24 June, a date which had become a red-letter one on his calendar

> "Tarbolton twenty-fourth of June,
> You'll find me in another tune."

on the day of the Grand Procession (and subsequent rejoicings at the Cross Keys)[8], he took what he thought was his last farewell from the Brethren. His feelings on that occasion may best be expressed in his own words.

> Adieu! a heart warm, fond adieu;
> Dear Brothers of the *Mystic Tie*!
> Ye favour' ye enlighten'd few,
> Companions of my social joy;
> Tho' I to foreign lands must hie,
> Pursuing Fortune's slidd'ry ba';
> With melting heart and brimful eye,
> I'll mind you still, tho' far awa.
>
> Oft have I met your social band,
> And spent the cheerful festive night;
> Oft, honour'd with supreme command,
> Presided o'er the *Sons of Light*;
> And by that *Hieroglyphic* bright,
> Which none but *Craftsmen* ever saw,
> Strong Mem'ry on my heart shall write
> These happy scenes, when far awa.

May Freedom, Harmony and Love,
Unite you in the *Grand Design*,
Beneath th' Omniscient Eye above –
The glorious *Architect Divine* –
That you may keep the *Unerring Line*,
Still rising by the *Plummet's Law*,
Till *Order* bright completely shine
Shall be my pray'r when far awa.

A last request permit me here,
When yearly ye assemble a'
One round, I ask it with a tear
To him, the Bard that's far awa.

By the inclusion of these verses in his Kilmarnock volume, the Bard proclaimed to the world at large that he was a Mason. That fact is well-known and well authenticated. What is not quite so well known, is the fact that the other man whose name appears on the title page, John Wilson, Printer, was also a Mason. That is an interesting circumstance. One would have to search a very long time indeed to find another volume of verse with the names of two masons on its title page. However, we mustn't make too much of this circumstance. Burns had not much choice. Wilson, in fact, was the only printer in Ayrshire and that they were both masons might well be a pure coincidence. So let us leave it at that! At this period of history, it was the usual thing for books to display on their title pages the names of at least four different people. In a book of poetry one would expect to find the name of the Poet, the name of the Poet's Patron, the name of the Poet's Publisher and the name of the Publisher's Printer. This volume has only two. Where are the other two? Where is the publisher – that astute man of business, with the book trade at his finger-ends, who will stand between the poet and the public, between the poet and the printer, and accept financial responsibility if the book is a failure. Here there is none. The Poet is his own publisher. That is another remarkable circumstance. Here we have a young man who has spent practically all of his life on a remote moorland farm, who had to start working at the age of eight and at fourteen to undertake the labour of a full grown man, who had never travelled more than a dozen miles from his own parish, who normally went about in home-made clothes with his boots caked with clay and cow-dung[9], who had never put his foot on a carpet or his hindquarters on an upholstered chair – this young man appears before the world as a publisher of his own poetry. That is something worth pondering.

The Publisher then drops out of the picture, but what of the Patron? Eighteenth Century authors, particularly poets, were usually miserable social outcasts, eking out a precarious existence in garrets or debtors' gaols. To appear in print they had to seek out some V.I.P. and on bended knee humbly to solicit his patronage. If his lordship was sufficiently condescending, he would stretch out a protecting arm, render what assistance was necessary and under his aegis the author was able to appear in public in an aura of respectability. The Patron's reward was an obsequious Dedication lauding him as a paragon on all the virtues.

This volume has no Dedication on the title pages, but on scanning the index the eye is arrested by the title of a poem, "A Dedication", toward the end of the book and on turning it up we find that it is one without a doubt. – "A Dedication to G. H., Esq." One wonders why it was inserted in such an unusual, such an unorthodox place, but then it is an unusual, unorthodox Dedication. The Author begins by warning the Patron that he is not to expect a "fleechin', fletherin' Dedication", that is to say there will be none of the flowery, flattering high-falutin' nonsense commonly employed in such effusions. No, the position is plain, he (the Patron), is a man who possesses that *sine qua non* of the 18th Century – a pedigree, whereas the Author has no such thing. (Not here, but elsewhere he had boasted that "his ancient but ignoble blood had poured through scoundrels since the flood"). The Patron is – well "just nae better than he should be". That being so, the deep obeisance appropriate to such occasions can be dispensed with. Then follows a long disquisition on divinity and morality (with special emphasis on the sin of hypocrisy), obscure to us, but full of meaning to the readers of that time and place. Then pulling himself up with a broad grin, the Poet exclaims:

> Your pardon Sir for this digression,
> I maist forgat my Dedication,
> But when Divinity comes cross me
> My readers then are sure to lose me."

Follows the Dedication proper, short, pithy, homely – finishing with

> "I will not wind a lang conclusion,
> With complimentary effusion,
> But whilst your wishes and endeavours,
> Are blest with Fortune's smiles and favours,
> I am, Dear Sir, with zeal most fervent,
> Your much indebted, humble servant."

At this point the Poet, obviously, should have signed off, but further thoughts crowd in. "Fortune's smiles" yes, but what if fortune should frown on the Patron. If by some "black mischance" cruel Want should overtake him to such an extent as would reduce him to the level of the Poet, what then? Finish then with "humble servant."

> If friendless, low, we meet together
> Then, Sir, your hand – my FRIEND and BROTHER."

Friend and Brother. In his voluminous private correspondence Robert Burns once only uses a masonic form of address. "My Friend and Brother." Here the two words are in large capitals, emphasised no doubt for the attention of the discerning, the "enlightened few".

Who was this G. H. Esq., here addressed in terms of mingled respect and jocular familiarity? The initials did not in any way conceal the identity of Gavin Hamilton, a solicitor, practising in the little village of Mauchline, about 5 miles from Kilmarnock. Gavin Hamilton was also factor or estate agent for the Earl of Loudon, who had large possessions in those parts. In the latter capacity, he was to all intents and purposes "the Laird" or squire of the locality and thus the outward

43

visible relationship between the Poet and Patron was the relationships of tenant and landlord. It is rather unusual to find a tenant addressing his landlord in public in such cordial terms. When that happens, we have to look for some other relationship between them. The circumstances under which this relationship of landlord and tenant arose, are interesting. Gavin Hamilton had leased from his principals the farm of Mossgiel outside the village, with the intention of running it as a hobby. Instead of occupying it, he suddenly and unaccountably let it *(sub. rosa)*, to the brothers Burns, Robert and Gilbert. That was a rather unbusiness-like transaction, not the kind of transaction one would expect on the part of a canny lawyer. The situation of the Burns brothers was notorious. All their lives they had laboured on their father's farm, forming, with the other members of the family, a team which had waged in a grinding never-ending struggle to keep the wolf from the door. The wolf had got inside the door. When Hamilton let the farm to them, their father was on his death bed, worn out with toil and disease and he was dying a broken-hearted man. Recently he had the humiliating experience of being "put to the drum", i.e., proclaimed throughout the countryside as a bankrupt and his possessions were sequestrated, pending an action in court by his landlord, who alleged that Burns was behind with his rent to the extent of £500. But for the fact that he was "*in extremis*" he would have suffered the crowning indignity of being flung into gaol, the fate of all in those days who were suspected of being unable to meet their financial obligations. Death or gaol, the landlord would sell them up lock, stock and barrel. That would mean the end of the Burns family as a unit. Old Mrs Burns would have to go on the parish and the sons and daughters would have to shoulder their little bundles and start tramping the roads in search of work, just as their father's family had done. For a proud and independent family which had stuck together through thick and thin, the prospect was black indeed. Between them and beggary, there was nothing but the power to labour with their hands. In this extremity, Gavin Hamilton lets a £90 a year farm (for the rent of which he would presumably be responsible personally), to the two elder sons knowing they had not a couple of bawbees to rub together. Why did he do so? Ask the biographers and you will get a dusty answer. They can see nothing unusual in the transaction.

No one can, of course, say with certainty why he abandoned his own tenancy in favour of a bankrupt family, but one might venture to suggest that a clue to this quixotic action may be found in the minute book of a local masonic lodge.

In the little village of Newmilns, Lodge Loudon Kilwinning met on 27 March 1786. Here is the minute

"Much to the satisfaction of the Lodge, Mr Robert Burns, Mossgiel Mauchline, introduced by the Right Worshipful, was admitted a member of this Lodge.
John Morton, merchant in Newmilns is answerable for Mr Robert Burns's admission money."

In passing let us pay tribute to Brother Morton, who stood up in Lodge as the guarantor for the payment of Mr Burns' 12/6d joining fee on that occasion. Now this minute is unusual in its departure from the normal dry matter-of-factness of the period. It registers an emotion – "much satisfaction". Much satisfaction, indeed, could be expected from the appearance of Mr Burns in any social gathering. No company could be dull when he was present. He was a boon companion – sociable to the nth degree – a live wire who could be reckoned on to "set the table in a roar".

The time was not far distant when some of the highest in the land were to confess that his amazing conversational powers had simply swept them off their feet. These humble brethren felt satisfaction in having such a man in their midst and, undoubtedly, that satisfaction was greatly enhanced by the circumstance that he was introduced by the Right Worshipful himself.

The Right Worshipful of that Lodge at that date was Gavin Hamilton. The Hamilton-Burns relationship, was the relationship between the Right Worshipful of one Lodge and the Depute Master of another.

The tie which bound them together was the Mystic Tie. Masonry had made it possible for the squire and ploughman to come together in a bond of brotherhood. Like the heroes of the Kipling ballad they had "looked each other in the eye and there they had found no fault". They were Friends and Brothers, and when one found himself in a position of acute distress, it is not incredible that the other stretched forth a helping hand.

Whatever the motive that impelled Hamilton to take Burns as a tenant, there can be little doubt regarding the effect of his action.

From the time he entered into the tenancy of Mossgiel and during the period of his tenancy, the poetical genius of Robert Burns burgeoned and blossomed in a manner which was truly amazing. No other period of his life is in any way comparable with those two years. In Mossgiel, he rose to his full stature as a great poet. At Mossgiel, he took his place in the immortal band. Can we say that this was a mere coincidence? Perhaps it was, but assuredly the action of Hamilton did contribute something.

In another way Hamilton, unconsciously and unwittingly, did contribute something to his remarkable outburst of poesy. His affairs provided the Bard with material upon which to exercise his peculiar genius.

We cannot here enter into details of Hamilton's quarrel with the Kirk Session of Mauchline. Burns himself had come under the lash of that caucus of tyrannical bigots and so far as we know he never lost a night's sleep over it, but when the "holy beagles" set out in full cry after his Friend and Brother, the effect on the Bard was electrical. He gave vent to his blazing indignation and emptied the vials of his scorn on the persecutors. The Hamilton affair was responsible for much of Burns' anti-clerical verse, which swept ecclesiastical tyranny from the face of Scotland in a blast of ridicule.

It is to Hamilton for instance, that we owe that remarkable piece of devastating satire "Holy Willie's Prayer". In it, we get a thumb-nail sketch of the Patron.

> Lord, mind Gau'n Hamilton's deserts,
>   He drinks and swears and plays at cartes,
> Yet has sae many taking arts,
>   Wi' great and sma'
> Frae God's ain Priest the people's hearts,
>   He steals awa.

Hamilton, by his easy going good nature and broad human outlook, had won the hearts of the people and the Kirk Session found that hard to forgive.

One further service performed by Hamilton remains to be mentioned. The biographers tell us, that when Burns disclosed his intention to leave Scotland for good, he was persuaded by his friends to print his poems. That is quite true, but it is not the whole truth. To that statement two words have to be added. He was persuaded by his "friends and brothers". In this matter, we have valuable evidence from his blood (and masonic) brother Gilbert, honest canny sober-sided Gilbert. Despite the wide gulf which separated them temperamentally, the two brothers worked together harmoniously. Day in, day out, they toiled in the fields and night slept in the same bed. Gilbert may therefore be presumed to know something of his mercurial brother's affairs. His statement is that "Mr Hamilton advised him to publish his poems". No doubt other voices were added, but undoubtedly Gavin Hamilton was the chief persuader. He was the man who talked Robert Burns into the venture which produced the Kilmarnock volume and with him lies the honour of having preserved the Bard from oblivion. Had he not done so, Burns would have left his native land a bitterly disappointed man and left behind him nothing but the reputation of a reckless scapegrace, "who had a lot to say for himself", whose conduct was not redeemed by a facility for stringing rhymes together. His memory would have died out in a generation. Many and many a genius has had to pass on without getting the recognition which his genius deserved and that would have been the fate of Robert Burns, but for the intervention of Brother Hamilton, backed by a few other members of the craft – Brother Bob Aiken and Brother John Ballantine (both of Lodge Ayr Kilwinning) to mention only two. To the former, the Bard dedicated his "Cottars Saturday Night" and to the latter "The Brigs of Ayr" and, as we have seen, his gratitude to Hamilton was manifested by the selection of that Brother as his patron – the man who had made his appearance as an author possible.

Thus, it comes about that we have Poet, Patron and Printer, all masons. Those three in collaboration may produce a volume of verse, but their efforts will come to naught unless they are backed and supported by the Public.

History is silent on the negotiations which took place between Poet and Printer. Wilson was a member of Lodge St John Kilwinning, Kilmarnock, in which the Poet was a well known visitor and latterly a member. Burns would seem to have found in Brother Johnny, a somewhat tough bargainer, judging by the little skit he wrote in course of the negotiations and slyly induced the unsuspecting Wilson to include in the volume.

> Hic Jacet. Wee Johnny.
> Whoe'er thou art; O Reader know,
> That Death has murdered Johnny[10],
> And here his body lies fu' low
> For saul, he ne'er had ony.

The Bard had a soul, a most unsordid soul and was not usually capable of appreciating the business point of view. To Brother Wilson, masonry was masonry, but business was business and he was not in the printing business for the fun of the thing. Producing a book, meant heavy initial outlay and what were the prospects of recoupment in a community where not one man in a thousand would think of buying a book of poetry in the course of his natural life. Brother Burns hadn't a bawbee to put down and was not, most definitely not, prepared to borrow. Nothing in the world would induce him to enter upon financial obligations involving the surrender of his independence. That being so, the only alternative was subscription. Could Brother Burns go out into the world and find some three or four hundred people who would give a written undertaking to purchase a book they had never seen, and thus guarantee the printer's oncost?

That must have been a poser for Brother Burns. The world he looked out upon, was not a place to inspire confidence. It was a hostile, an unfriendly world. Throughout the negotiations, his personal troubles had reached such a pitch that he was almost demented. Nevertheless, in spite of everything, he reckoned that he still had a few friends on whom he could rely in his extremity and he had a shrewd idea where he would find them.

It is unfortunate that the subscription list for the Kilmarnock volume has disappeared. With it, one might speak with greater certainty. All that we have is an incomplete part of the account rendered by John Wilson, Printer to Robert Burns, Poet. It contains the names of ten persons to whom supplies of the book were issued. The total edition was 612 copies and Wilson declined to lift a finger till he had 350 subscribers. Then ten who can almost all be identified as "Friends and Brothers" took between them 455 copies. That little group of Ayrshire brethren therefore secured the necessary signatures to ensure publication. Masons produced the book and masons sold it. We are entitled to claim that it was a Craft effort. The Kilwinning Masons did not make Robert Burns a genius, but they saw to it that his genius was established and recognised.

The Poems were an instantaneous and outstanding success and Brother Burns proudly assumed the title of "The Ayrshire Bard", but from "Ayrshire Bard" to "Caledonia's Bard" is a far cry indeed. How the latter title came to be conferred upon him in the bosom of a Masonic Lodge in a Masonic Toast proposed by the Grand Master and how it came about that the second edition of the "Poems" bore on the title pages the names of five Brothers in the Craft – that is a story which will have to wait.

EDITOR'S FOOTNOTES TO CHAPTER SIX

1. From his description of Tarbolton one must assume the Author never visited the Village and that he had no knowledge of its Civil and Ecclesiastical History. To any reader of this work I would commend for his/her perusal Helen Stein's admirable booklet – *Tarbolton: Its History and Associations*.
2. Tarboltonians.
3. Was this really the reason why Lodge Mother Kilwinning withdrew and did not rejoin Grand Lodge until 1807?
4. An absurd suggestion. Did Brother Sclater ever read Lodge St David's Minutes?
5. The Minute calls it a "juncheon".
6. To the Farming Community "the young ploughman" would equate with a hired servant and not the farmer's son.
7. From 1784-1788, 4 years.
8. In 1786 the Lodge was meeting in "Manson's Inn".
9. Why such a description? Is it possible to work on a farm without muddy boots etc.?
10. Was this really John Wilson? Eminent Burns Students – e.g. Dr William Wallace and Dr D. McNaught – shared the view that a Mauchline grocer of the same name was more likely to be subject of the Epitaph.

Part Two

Chapter Seven

VISITS TO EDINBURGH: HIGHLAND AND BORDER TOURS

The decision of Burns in 1786 to publish his poems – *The Kilmarnock Edition* – was a conscious one. That decision and the subsequent events arising therefrom are best related in the Poet's own words. In his Autobiographical Note to Dr Moore he wrote:

"When my father died, his all went among the hell-hounds that prowl in the kennel of justice; but we made a shift to collect a little money in the family amongst us, with which, to keep us together, my brother and I took (Mossgiel) a neighbouring Farm. My brother wanted my hair-brained imagination, as well as my social and amorous madness; but, in good sense, and every sober qualification, he was far my superior.

"I entered on this farm with a full resolution, 'Come, go to, I will be wise!' I read farming books; I calculated crops; I attended markets; and, in short, in spite of 'the devil, and the world, and the flesh', I believe I should have been a wise man; but the first year, from unfortunately buying bad seed, the second, from the late harvest, we lost half our crops. This overset all my wisdom, and I returned, 'like the dog to his vomit, and the sow that was washed to her wallowing in the mire'.

"I now began to be known in the neighbourhood as a maker of rhymes. The first of my poetic offspring that saw the light, was a burlesque lamentation on a quarrel between two Reverend Calvinists, both of them *dramatis personae* in my 'Holy Fair'. I had a notion myself, that the piece has some merit; but, to prevent the worst, I gave a copy of it to a friend who was very fond of such things, and told him I could not guess who was the author of it, but that I thought it pretty clever. With a certain description of the clergy, as well as laity, it met with a roar of applause. 'Holy Willie's Prayer' next made its appearance, and alarmed the kirk-session so much, that they held several meetings to look over their spiritual artillery, if haply any of it might be pointed against profane rhymers. Unluckily for me, my wanderings led me on another side, within point blank shot of their heaviest metal. This is the unfortunate story that gave rise to the printed poem 'The Lament'. This was a most melancholy affair, which I cannot yet bear to reflect on, and had very nearly given me one or two of the principal qualifications for a place among those who have lost the chart, and mistaken the reckoning of rationality. I gave up my part of the farm to my brother; in truth, it was only nominally mine; and made what little preparation was in my power for Jamaica. But, before leaving my native country forever, I resolved to publish my poems. I weighed my productions as impartially as was in my power: I thought they had merit; and it was a delicious idea that I should be called a clever fellow, even though it should never reach my ears a poor negro driver; – or perhaps a victim to that inhospitable clime, and gone to the world of the spirits! I can truly say, that *pauvre inconnu* as I then was, I had pretty nearly as high an idea of myself and of my works as I have at this moment, when the public has decided in their favour. It ever was my opinion, that the mistakes and blunders, both in a rational and religious point of view, of which we see thousands daily guilty, are owing to their ignorance of themselves. – To know myself, had been all along my constant study. I weighed myself alone; I balanced myself with others; I watched every means of information, to see how much ground I occupied as a man and as a poet; I studied assiduously nature's design in my formation – where the lights and shades in my character were intended. I was pretty confident my poems would meet with some applause; but, at the worst, the roar of the Atlantic would deafen the voice of censure, and the novelty of West-Indian scenes make me forget neglect. I threw off six hundred copies, of which I had got subscriptions for about three hundred and fifty. – My vanity was highly gratified by the reception I met from the public; and, besides, I pocketed, all expenses deducted, nearly twenty pounds. The sum came very seasonably, as I was thinking of indenting myself, for want of money to procure my passage. As soon as I was master of nine guineas, the price of wafting me to the torrid zone, I took a steerage-passage in the first ship that was to sail from the Clyde; for

'Hungry ruin had me in the wind'

"I had been for some days skulking from covert to covert, under all the terrors of a jail; as some ill-advised people had uncoupled the merciless pack of the law at my heels. I had taken the last farewell of my few friends; my chest was on the road to Greenock; I had composed the last song I should ever measure in Caledonia, 'The gloomy night is gathering fast', when a letter from Dr Blackwood to a friend of mine[1], overthrew all my schemes, by opening new prospects to my poetic ambition. The Dr belonged to a set of critics, for whose applause I had not dared to hope. His opinion, that I would meet with encouragement in Edinburgh for a second edition, fired me so much, that away I posted for that city, without a single acquaintance, or a single letter of introduction. The baneful star which had so long shed its blasting influence in my zenith, for once made a revolution to the nadir; and a kind Providence placed me under the patronage of one of the noblest of men, the Earl of Glencairn. *Oublie moi, Grand Dieu, si jamais je l'oublie!*

"I need relate no farther. At Edinburgh I was in a new world; I mingled among many classes of men, but all of them new to me, and I was all attention to catch the characters and manners 'living as they rise'."

His Reception in Edinburgh

Let Brother Fred Belford now take up the story.

Burns presided at a meeting of his Lodge on 10 November 1786, soon after which he set his face towards Edinburgh, reaching there on 28 November and taking up his residence with his friend John Richmond in Baxter's Close, Lawnmarket. In the metropolis he was to spend some of the happiest moments of his life, and these were closely bound up with Freemasonry. Two days after his arrival the Grand Lodge of Scotland celebrated the Festival of Saint Andrew. The Brethren assembled in the aisle of St Giles and walked in procession to St Andrew's Church, where a Masonic service was conducted. Burns may have been in that procession as invitations were issued to Brethren of country Lodges requesting their presence at the function. Shortly after his arrival in the city he was introduced to Lodge Canongate Kilwinning by Brother James Dalrymple of Orangefield[2] near Ayr, and who had previously known the poet. He is reputed to have attended a meeting of this Lodge on 7 December, but Brother D. Murray Lyon does not admit to definite evidence on the point. If he was there, and whether or not, he met Lord Glencairn and the Hon. Henry Erskine, both introduced by Brother Dalrymple. Of these three Brethren Burns writes in terms of the highest praise. In conversation with his friend Gavin Hamilton the same evening, he says:

"I am in a fair way to becoming as eminent as Thomas à Kempis or John Bunyan . . . My Lord Glencairn and the Dean of Faculty, Mr H. Erskine, have taken me under their wing; and by all probability I shall soon be the tenth worthy, and the eighth wise man of the world . . . I have met in Mr Dalrymple, of Orangefield, what Solomon emphatically calls 'A friend that sticketh closer than a brother.'"

The Earl of Glencairn never lost interest in Burns. He introduced him to Creech the publisher, secured the patronage of the Caledonian Hunt, did everything in his power to obtain subscribers among the nobility, and used his influence of get Burns

51

into the Excise. Burns was not the man to allow this kindness to pass without showing his appreciation. Some three years later Glencairn died, and when the poet learned of this he wrote to the factor in these words:

> "Dare I trouble you to let me know privately before the day of interment, and I may cross the country and steal among the crowd to pay a tear to the slight sight of my ever revered benefactor?"

And in addition to this he composed in his "Lament for James, Earl of Glencairn" one of the finest stanzas he ever wrote:

> "The bridegroom may forget the bride
> Was made his wedded wife yesteen;
> The monarch may forget the crown
> That on his head an hour has been;
> The mother may forget the bairn
> That smiles sae sweetly on her knee;
> But I'll remember thee, Glencairn,
> And a' that thou hast done for me!"

In Edinburgh he was to find many of the literati who thought highly of him. Principal Robertson, for example, owned that he scarcely ever met any man whose conversation displayed more intellectual vigour. Dugald Stewart's reference to him has already been noted. Dalzel, Professor of Greek in Edinburgh University says:

> "We have a poet in town just now, whom everybody is taking notice of – a ploughman from Ayrshire – a man of unquestionable genius. He runs the risk of being spoiled by the excessive attention paid him just now by persons of all ranks. Those who know him best say he has too much good sense to allow himself to be spoiled."

Burns' fame was now rapidly growing and he threw himself zealously into the work of publishing a second and enlarged volume of his poems. He was to find that the Masonic associations which had proved so helpful in the issue of his Kilmarnock Edition were to stand him in good stead again. These friends were practically all members of Lodge Canongate Kilwinning.

He definitely visited Lodge St Andrew on 12 January 1787, on the occasion of a visitation from Grand Lodge when the Grand Master Charteris unexpectedly gave the toast "Caledonia and Caledonia's Bard, Brother Burns". The following day Brother John Ballantine of Ayr received this letter from the poet describing his visit to the Lodge:

> "I went to a Mason Lodge yesternight where the Most Worshipful Grand Master Charteris and all the Grand Lodge of Scotland visited. The meeting was most numerous and elegant; all the different Lodges about town were present in all their pomp. The Grand Master, who presided with great solemnity, and honour to himself as a Gentleman and Mason, among other general toasts gave 'Caledonia and Caledonia's Bard, Brother Burns', which rung through the whole Assembly with multiplied honours and repeated acclamations. As I had no idea such a thing would happen, I was downright thunderstruck, and trembling in every nerve made the best return in my power. Just as I finished, some of the Grand Officers said so loud as I could hear, with a most comforting accent, 'Very well indeed', which set me something to rights again."

The interior of the Chapel of St John looking east.

The interior of the Chapel of St John looking south.

Key of the painting by Brother Stewart Watson (between pages 4-5).

0. Alexander Fergusson, Esq., of Craigdarroch – R.W.M.
1. The Hon. Francis Charteris (Lord Elcho) – Grand Master.
2. James Sandilands, 9th Lord Torphichen – R.W.M. 1787-8.
3. Archibald, 11th Earl of Eglinton.
4. James Cunningham, Earl of Glencaairn.
5. David. Earl of Buchan.
6. Charles More, of the Royal Bank of Scotland – Depute Master.
7. Patric Millar, of Dalswinton.
8. James Dalrymple, of Orangefield.
9. Sir John Whitefoord, of Ballock-myle.
10. Sir William Forbes, of Pitsligo, Bart.
11. John Mercer, Secretary.
12. William Mason – Grand Secretary.
13. Robert Meikle (absent).
14. James Burnet, Advocate (Lord Monboddo).
15. The Hon. Henry Erskine, Dean of Faculty – R.W.M. 1780.
16. George Spankie, Treasurer.
17. Fletcher Norton, Baron Norton of the Exchequer.
18. Henry Mackenzie, Author of "The Man of Feeling."
19. The Hon. William Gordon (Lord Kenmure).
20. Alexander Cunnignham, Jeweller.
21. William Dunbar – Senior Warden. R.W.M. 1788.
22. Kenneth Love, Tailor and Clothier.
23. William Nichol, of the High School.
24. William Cruickshank, of the High School.
25. Louis Caauvin, French Teacher.
26. Allan Masterton, Composer of Music.
27. Signor Stabilini, Violinist.
28. James Tytler, Author, etc.
29. Thomas Neil, Precentor of Old Tolbooth Church.
30. John Dhu – Grand Tyler.
31. Alexander Campbell, Organist, etc.
32. John Campbell, Teacher of Music
33. Samuel Clark, Organist of Cowgate Chapel.
34. Geordie Cranstoun, Vocalist.
35. J. G. Schetky, Musician.
36. Professor Dugald Stewart.
37. William Creech, Publisher.
38. Peter Williamson, (Aberdonian).
39. William Smellie, Publisher.
40. Peter Hill, Bookseller.
41. Sir James Hunter Blair – Grand Treasurer.
42. Francis, 7th Lord Napier.
43. James Boswell of Auchinleck, Biographer of Johnson.
44. Alexander Nasmyth, Limner.
45. James Johnson, Music-Seller, etc.
46. Captain Francis Grose, F.A.S., of London and Perth.
47. James Gregory, M.D.
48 Alexander Wood, Surgeon.
49. David Ramsay, Journalist.
50. John Gray, W.S., City Clerk.
51. John Millar, Advocate, The Historian
52. Captain Fr. Bartlet, of Milton House.
53. Robert Ainslie, Writer to the Signet.
54. William Woods, Tragedian.
55. A Visiting Brother.
56. The Tyler.
57. Figure representing *Secrecy*
58. Figure representing the *Light of Masonry.*
59. Portrait of William St. Clair of Rosslyn.
60. Henry Sedgefield, Royal Navy.

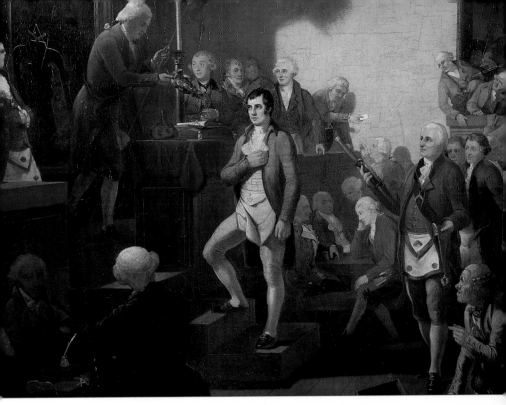

A close-up study of the painting by Brother Stewart Watson.

A page from the Sederant book of Lodge St Andrew, No. 179 (Dumfries).

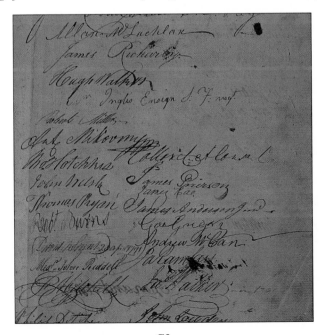

C3

The painting by Brother Stewart Watson entitled "The Inauguration

ns as Poet Laureate of Lodge Canongate Kilwinning, 1st March 1787".

A wall-plaque at Eyemouth Masonic Hall.

The interior of the meeting place of Lodge St Ebbe, No. 70, looking east.

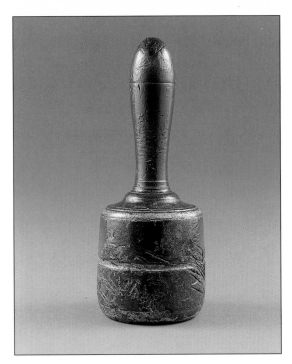

The Maul from Lodge St Andrew, No. 179.

Founder Member's Jewel of Lodge Robert Burns Initiated, No. 1781, Founded 1989.

Founder Master's Jewel of Lodge Robbie Burns, No. 860 (Western Australia), Founded 1897.

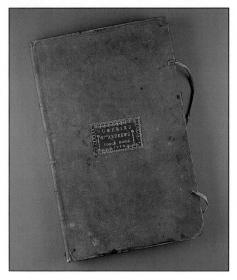

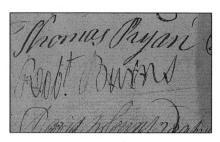

The Sederant book of Lodge St Andrew, No. 179.

The signature of Robert Burns in the Lodge St Andrew, No. 179, Sederant book.

Founder Member's Jewel of Lodge Robert Burns, No. 1542 (Natal), Founded 1958.

Founder Member's Jewel of Lodge Burns Dundonald, No. 1759, Founded 1985.

The Cottage at Alloway where Robert Burns was born on 25th January 1759.

The kitchen of the cottage.

The interior of the Bachelor's Club; Robert and his brother, Gilbert, were Founder Members of this Club.

William Creech, the Publisher of Burns' Edinburgh Edition, who is shown in the Stewart Watson Painting.

The Publishing House of Creech, situated in the centre of the High Street in Edinburgh.

Here Lies
ROBERT FERGUSSON POET
Born September. 5. 1751.
Died October 16" 1774.
No sculptur'd Marble here nor pompous lay
No storied Urn nor animated Bust
This simple Stone directs Pale Scotia's way
To pour her Sorrows o'er her Poets Dust

1850

The gravestone for Burns' friend, Robert Fergusson, and the inscription which states that Burns received permission to pay for, and erect, a stone over his fellow Poet's unmarked grave in the Canongate Kirkyard.

By Special grant of the Managers to ROBERT BURNS who erected this Stone this Burial place is to remain for ever Sacred to the memory of ROBERT FERGUSSON

The Memorial to our National Bard, situated near the Calton Hill in Edinburgh.

The plaque on the Chair in Loudoun Kilwinning No. 51 reads: "This Chair was occupied by Brother Robert Burns, Mossgeil, Mauchline on the date when he was made an Affiliate Member of Lodge Loudoun Newmilns Kilwinning No. 51. 27th March 1786."

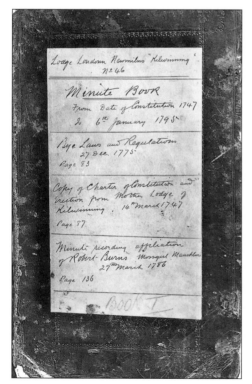

The Minute Book of Lodge Loudoun Kilwinning No. 51.

The Minute which records the Affiliation of Robert Burns reads: "When at same time much to the satisfaction of the Lodge, Mr. Robert Burns, Mossgeil, Mauchline, introduced by the Right Worshipful, was admitted as a member of this Lodge . . . John Morton, Merchant in Newmilns, is answerable for Mr. Burns' admission."

On the list of members, Robert Burns is designated as follows: "Robert Burns, Poet".

The Procession of Lodge St James (K

) of Tarbolton No. 135 in the 1830s.

The interior of Lodge St James (Kilwinning) Tarbolton No. 135 with a statue of its most famous Brother overseeing the Chair on which he sat as Depute Master, the gavel and the candlesticks which were in a similar position in his time.

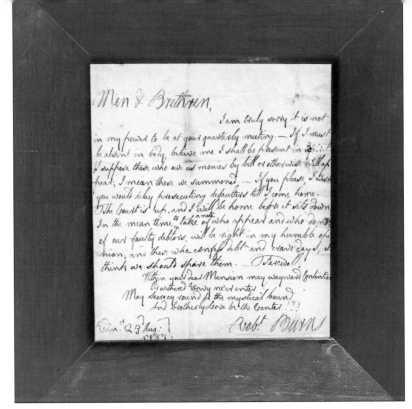

The original "Letter of Apology" sent by Brother Robert Burns to his Brethren on 23rd August 1787.

The address on the package to "The Right Worshipful St James's Lodge, Tarbolton, c/o James Mason, Inn-keeper, Tarbolton".

The Globe Tavern in Dumfries, described by Robert Burns as his "favourite Howff".

Burns' home in Mill Street, Dumfries where he died on 21st July 1796.

Portrait of John Wilson, a member of Lodge St John Kilwinning, Kilmarnock, No. 22, a Publisher in Kilmarnock who, in 1786, published the first edition of Burns' Poems "Chiefly in the Scottish Dialect".

The latest statue of Robert Burns and the Printer of his Kilmarnock Edition was unveiled by the Princess Royal on 27th September 1995 in the Town Centre of Kilmarnock. The statue is positioned in such a way that Robert Burns is looking towards the Ayreshire heartland, while John Wilson (to the rear of the Poet) is facing in the direction of Edinburgh.

15

Many statues appear throughout the world to the memory of Caledonia's Bard. This statue is in Vancouver, British Columbia.

Two weeks afterwards, on 1 February, we find him in Lodge Canongate Kilwinning, surrounded by some of the literary personalities of Edinburgh, and there he was affiliated as set forth in the following short Minute:

> "The Right Worshipful Master (Alexander Fergusson of Craigdarroch) having observed that Brother Burns was at present in the Lodge, who is well known as a great poetic writer, and for a late publication of his works, which have been universally commended, and submitted that he should be assumed a member of this Lodge, which was unanimously agreed to, and he was assumed accordingly".

The Minute concludes thus:

> "Having spent the evening in a very social manner, as the meetings of the Lodge always have been, it was adjourned till next monthly meeting."

and it was at this meeting on 1 March that Burns is supposed to have been installed as Poet Laureate. The Minute of 1 February went upon the Lodge Book, and it is preserved today in the Lodge among its choicest treasures. The meeting on 1 February was, so far as is known, the last Masonic meeting attended by Burns in Edinburgh, if we omit the ceremony of the Poet Laureateship on 1 March, about which there has been so much dispute. The matter has never been satisfactorily cleared up. Lodge books in those days were very imperfectly kept. Many of the Minutes were not even signed. For example, there is no Minute in the St Andrew's Lodge Books that Burns was ever in that Lodge, and his visit there might never have been remembered had he not happened to refer to it in the letter already quoted to one of his friends.

With regard to the much discussed meeting of Lodge Canongate Kilwinning on 1 March 1787, it has been assumed that the business which was to have come before the meeting was in the first place to send a letter of congratulation to the Prince of Wales, who had on 6 February been initiated into the mysteries of Freemasonry at the Star and Garter, London, and secondly to confer a mark of respect on Robert Burns. But the Minute in question as it appears in the Canongate Kilwinning records reads:

> "St John's Chapel, 1st March 1787. – The Lodge being duly constituted, it was reported that since last meeting" (and here follows the names of newly made Entered Apprentices and Fellows of Craft) "no other business being before the meeting the Lodge adjourned."

No word here of Burns' installation as Poet Laureate nor of any congratulatory epistle to the Prince of Wales.

Was he referring to the Laureateship when he penned the following lines in acknowledgement of a present from a friend?

> "But Latin Willie's reek no raise (Willie Nichol)
> He'd seen that nicht *Rab crown'd wi' bays.*"

It would appear that as far as Lodge Canongate is concerned the first reference to Burns' inauguration to the Poet Laureateship was not until 1815, when the Brethren were asked to subscribe to the fund for the erection of the Mausoleum of Burns who, they said, "had been Poet Laureate to the Lodge", this being followed in 1835 when James Hogg, the Ettrick Shepherd, was elected to succeed Burns as

Poet Laureate, acknowledged the honour conferred upon him as well as the compliment of being Burns' successor. The Brethren drank to the memory of Burns as "the last Poet Laureate of the Lodge". If any of those who were members of the Lodge in 1787 were present on either or both of these dates they must have known the facts. Certain it is that the statements were never contradicted.

An interesting correspondence between Brother H. C. Peacock, Secretary of the Lodge, and Brother D. Murray Lyon is to be found in *The History of the Lodge Canongate Kilwinning, No. 2,* by Allan Mackenzie, R.W.M., in 1883-1887, regarding the controversy.

The Edinburgh Edition of Burns' poems was published on 21 April 1787, from the publishing shop of Mr Creech, in the Luckenbooths. It was in a handsome octavo volume, price five shillings. Creech's advertisement contained the following note:

"As the book is published for the sole benefit of the author, it is requested that subscribers will send for their copies: and none will be delivered without money."

The Kilmarnock Preface was abandoned and in its place appeared a

DEDICATION
TO THE NOBLEMEN AND GENTLEMEN
OF THE CALEDONIAN HUNT

and then follows the Preface by Burns. The list of Subscribers extended to over thirty-eight pages comprising 1,500 persons subscribing for 2,800 copies. Many of them were members of Lodge Canongate Kilwinning. Smellie, his printer, Creech, his publisher, and Naysmith, who provided the frontispiece to his works, were all Masons. In that connection it has been said that "surely never book came out of a more Masonic laboratory". It was, too, his Brother Mason, John Ballantyne of Ayr who, hearing that poverty prevented the publication of a second edition of his poems, offered to lend him the money required for the purpose.

"Affliction's sons are brothers in distress;
A brother to relieve, how exquisite the bliss."

There is no doubt that his connection with Freemasonry in Edinburgh was the most interesting and to him the most enjoyable period of his life, and it was during the few months spent there that his genius was appreciated and rewarded.

Border and Highland Tours

After having spent about five months in the capital he set out on 6 May 1787 on a tour to the South of Scotland with Mr Robert Ainslie, a young lawyer, to whom he had been introduced at a Masonic meeting. They visited a number of interesting spots and met several distinguished people. On 7 May they reached Coldstream and crossed the border into England. Burns' love for his native land overcame him here and he could not refrain from uttering aloud, with deep emotion and devotion, the two concluding stanzas of "The Cottar's Saturday Night", four of the lines being:

"O Scotia! my dear, my native soil!
For whom my warmest wish to Heaven is sent!
Long may thy hardy sons of rustic toil
Be blest with health and peace and sweet content!"

On 18 May they arrived at Eyemouth where, through the influence of their host, a meeting of the Lodge was convened for the next day, and there Burns and Ainslie were made Royal Arch Masons, as set forth in the following Minute:

> "Eyemouth, 19th May 1787
> "At a general encampment held . . ." in Lodge St Ebbe, "the following Brethren were made Royal Arch Masons – namely Robert Burns . . . and Robert Ainslie . . . Robert Ainslie paid one guinea admission dues: but on account of R. Burns's remarkable poetical genius, the encampment unanimously agreed to admit him gratis, and considered themselves honoured by having a man of such shining abilities for one of their companions."

The members of the Lodge forming this "general encampment" secured an English Charter some three months later authorising them to be erected into a Royal Arch Chapter, bearing the name "Land of Cakes", No. 52, on the English Roll. The Chapter is now Scottish, No. 15.

Having parted with Ainslie he crossed the north of England to Dumfries, where he stayed two days and was presented with the freedom of the burgh. Ayr and Mossgiel were reached on 9 June and ten days later he was re-elected Depute Master of his Lodge, but there is no record of his being at the meeting and the Minute is unsigned. Lodge St James sometimes met by deputation at Mauchline. On 25 July he presided at a meeting there, honorary membership being conferred on several well-known Masons, including Professor Dugald Stewart, who had on more than one occasion befriended the poet.

In the early days of August Burns returned to Edinburgh to settle with his publisher. An important meeting of his Lodge was due, and he found himself unable to be present. He accordingly sent the following letter to his Tarbolton Lodge, addressed "Men and Brethren" and with the date "Edinburgh, 23 August 1787:

> "I am truly sorry it is not in my power to be at your quarterly meeting. If I must be absent in body, believe me I shall be present in spirit. I suppose those who owe us monies, by bill or otherwise, will appear – I mean those we summoned. If you please, I wish you would delay prosecuting defaulters till I come home. The court is up, and I will be home before it sits down. In the meantime to take a note of who appear and who do not, of our faulty debtors, will be right in my humble opinion, and those who confess debt and crave days, I think we should spare them. Farewell!

> Within your dear Mansion may wayward Contention
> Or withered Envy ne'er enter;
> May Secrecy round be the mystical bound,
> And brotherly Love be the Center!!!
> ROBERT BURNS."

The quatrain above it will be recalled was the last of the verses he wrote to Lodge Kilmarnock Kilwinning on his receiving honorary membership there. One word only was changed, viz.: "your" replacing "their" in the first line.

Two days later he set out on his Highland tour with Willie Nicol, immortalised as having "brewed a peck o' maut", said to be the greatest drinking song in any language. They reached beyond Inverness, travelling in all nearly 600 miles over a period of twenty-two days, and meeting many Masonic Brethren en route. Tradition has it that he was made an honorary member of Lodge Ancient Brazen, No. 17, Linlithgow, but there is no record of this having taken place. Lodge Stirling Ancient, No. 30, also believes that he attended a meeting of the Brethren and entered his name in the Attendance Book. This register used to be displayed to visitors, but on one occasion it was found that the page containing the poet's signature had been removed, and at a subsequent date the register too disappeared. This would almost indicate that he was in reality a visitor there. Their arrival in Edinburgh on 16 September completed the tour.

Burns spent the winter in the Capital prodding his publisher for a settlement. When this was squared he found himself enriched to the extent of £500. He was also in communication with Brother Patrick Millar of Dalswinton for a lease of the farm of Ellisland, and at the same time was seeking, through the good offices of one of his brother Masons, an appointment in the Excise. There is very little documentary evidence to show that he interested himself in Masonry during this second Edinburgh period, though it has been asserted that he attended many meetings during these five months. On one occasion he states in an undated letter that "To-night the Grand Master and Lodge of Masons appear at the Theatre in form. I am determined to go to the play . . . I will call on you a few minutes before the Theatre opens." Members of the Craft were patrons of the Drama and when a particular play was on they were wont to appear in full Masonic regalia.

Burns returned to Mossgiel in March 1788, married Jean Armour in April, and lent his brother Gilbert £200 to ease the condition of his widowed mother and her family. He attended his Lodge on 7 and 23 May, the latter occasion being the last time he signed the Minute as Depute Master. It is reputed that he foregathered with the Brethren on 24 June, on the occasion of the annual Masonic procession. A few days before, on 13 June, he had taken possession of Ellisland, but does not seem to have been enamoured with the idea of residing in Dumfriesshire, for in a letter to his friend Hugh Parker, lamenting the fact that he was missing his Ayrshire friends, he pens a verse concluding with:

> "Tarbolton, twenty-fourth of June,
> Ye'll find me in a better tune."

Another fact of regret to him was that there was not a "kenn'd face" in the district except his auld mare, Jenny Geddes:

> "Dowie she saunters doon Nithside
> And aye a westlin' leuk she throws
> While tears hap ower her auld broon nose."

On 24 June James Findlay, a fellow exciseman, was appointed Depute Master in succession to the poet, the Master being James Dalrymple of Orangefield, who has already been referred to as befriending Burns while in Edinburgh.

He paid flying visits to Mauchline on 21 October and 11 November, when his Lodge met under his presidency. This was the last meeting of Lodge St James he attended and his association with this Lodge which he so much adorned was at an end.

EDITOR'S FOOTNOTES TO CHAPTER SEVEN
1. Rev George Lawrie, Minister of Parish.
2. A member of Lodge St James No. 135 and later its Master.

Chapter Eight

ROBERT BURNS AND FREEMASONRY IN EDINBURGH

By the late Brother Dr R. T. Halliday, Past Grand Warden.

Taking a comprehensive view, the Masonic career of Robert Burns from his initiation at Tarbolton on 4 July 1781 till his death at Dumfries on 21 July 1796, may be divided into three stages. These are unequal in point of time and importance; nor are they distinctive periods as they dovetail into one another. Yet they have each their own significance. In the first we have the humble ploughman in the natural rural element of Ayrshire circles, hard pressed to maintain his own independence and that of his father's family, but surrounded by boon companions of a jovial country brotherhood. During this stage all his active Masonic work was done. In the second we find him in Edinburgh in a wholly different, and to him unnatural, atmosphere, lionised by the society of the day as the latest curiosity of that Metropolis, and flaunted for a time by Masonic associates of a quite dissimilar type. It was a brief but hectic interlude not inaptly described as "the circumstance of an opportunist", and though given a posthumous Masonic importance wholly unwarranted by facts, it involved no Masonic work of any kind. In the third stage the bard was back for a spell to the plough, tired and worried both physically and mentally, finally taking an official post which he had vainly calculated would bring him independence. Here he was again in his real Masonic element, but his day was far spent and his Masonic work practically over.

The Ayrshire period I have dealt with in an earlier paper. During this period Burns published "Poems, chiefly in the Scottish dialect", the first or Kilmarnock edition of his works, and for this the Fraternity in Ayrshire were in large measure responsible. The second stage, the visits of the Bard to the Scottish Metropolis and his Masonic doings and interests there, was a natural though unforeseen corollary which merits some special reference. The third stage may claim a like attention at some future date.

His initial venture in publication provided Burns with a sadly-needed £20 with which he made preparation for his intended departure to Jamaica in the autumn of 1786, and, but for a series of accidental happenings which postponed his sailing week after week, Burns might even then have been lost to Scotland. But "the best laid schemes o' mice and men gang aft agley". The delay gave time for more mature consideration and the decision to go to Edinburgh resulted.

Burns had several impelling reasons for that decision. The success of his first edition imbued him with the desire for a second, and we learn from his own pen of his futile endeavour to issue this in Ayrshire. But the poems had prompted Dr Thomas Blacklock to suggest that a further edition should be issued from Edinburgh; and this encouragement from "one of a set of critics for whose applause I had not even dared to hope" stimulated Burns to consider this proposal seriously. There was also some expectation, to which at that time he had not given much heed, that influence might be available there to secure for him a position in the Excise Service. But strongest of all was his sense of his responsibilities to Jean Armour who had borne him twins on 3 September. He had ever a commendable feeling of moral responsibility for his offspring. In a letter to Robert Aiken citing his uncertainties, disappointment, pride, remorse and general wretchedness, he wrote, "All these reasons urge me to go abroad, and to all these reasons I have only one answer, the feelings of a father. This overbalances everything that can be laid in the scale against it." He left Mossgiel on 27 November and reached Edinburgh the following day.[1]

The move to Edinburgh for a man of Burns' temperament was a dangerous and fateful hazard. The fame of his poems had preceded him and he was introduced into clubs such as the Crochallan Fencibles and social circles such as the Caledonian Hunt, where in that era of hard drinking and dissipation many would have completely lost their heads. "The Edinburgh of Boswell, Burns and Scott," wrote Professor Grierson, "was a centre of dissipation – drunken, immoral and pious, the different qualities blended sometimes in the most singular fashion." And Scott determined from his own close observation that his sons should never settle in Edinburgh if he could help it. Burns, however, kept steadily before him the main purport of his journey and set about the consummation of that business without delay. His Masonic associations again proved of value. James Dalrymple of Orangefield[2], a prominent Ayrshire Freemason, introduced him to the Earl of Glencairn and through him he met those "other luminaries in that galaxy of Scottish Craftsmen of which he for a time formed the centre of attraction" (Murray Lyon's History). By 7 December he was able to write to Gavin Hamilton, "My Lord Glencairn and the Dean of Faculty, Mr H. Erskine, have taken me under their wing. Through my Lord's influence it is inserted in the records of the Caledonian Hunt that they universally, one and all, subscribe for the second edition."

Mackenzie in his history of Lodge Canongate Kilwinning published in 1888, makes the assertion that "the first Lodge to which he (Burns) paid a visit was Canongate Kilwinning on 7 December, and after leaving it that night he wrote to his friend Gavin Hamilton." There is no record in the minute book of the Lodge of his presence nor does Burns mention such a meeting in his correspondence which at this time was voluminous and detailed. Where Mackenzie gleaned his information he does not state. But we know the source of this and other myths of the Bard's sojourn in Edinburgh to be Marshall's book, "A Winter with Robert Burns", probably the most unreliable concoction ever penned about him. Nor is Mackenzie trustworthy in other matters of detail. There are two inaccuracies in the opening paragraph of his chapter dealing with Burns. He notes that Burns was entered in Lodge St Davids in 1781 and in 1784 elected Depute Master. The name of the Lodge is St David and Burns never held office therein. He was one of the seceders who re-established the older Lodge St James, now No. 135, and in St James as Depute Master he "Presided o'er the Sons of Light". Here all his Ayrshire Masonic work was done. Brother D. Murray Lyon states that "an examination of the Canongate minutes shows that during Burns' residence in Edinburgh 1786-87, the Lodge held only three meetings and at only one is Burns recorded as being present." This effectively disposes of the mendacious phrases "He was the life of the Lodge", and "the seat he always resorted to".

The first Lodge he actually visited was St Andrew, now No. 48, and in a letter to James Ballantine, dated 14 January, he makes extended reference to this visit. "I went to a mason-lodge yesternight, where Most Worshipful Grand Master Charters[3] and all the Grand Lodge of Scotland visited. The meeting was numerous and elegant; all the different lodges about town were present in all their pomp. The Grand Master, who presided with great solemnity and honour to himself as a gentleman and a mason, among other general toasts gave "Caledonia and Caledonia's Bard, Brother Burns", which rung through the whole assembly with multiplied honours and repeated acclamations. As I had no idea such a thing would happen I was downright thunderstruck, and trembling in every nerve made the best return in my power. Just as I had finished some of the Grand Officers said, so loud that I could hear, 'Very well, indeed' which set me something to rights again." The argument has been advanced that this incident is not recorded in the minute of the St Andrew meeting; a statement which is strictly correct. The minute records the visit of the Grand Master and the business transacted; toasts follow at "Harmony" which it is unusual to record in minutes.

An outstanding Masonic incident occurred a fortnight later when Burns paid his sole-recorded visit to Lodge Canongate Kilwinning on 1 February, which was duly chronicled as business in its minute book. The minute of that meeting is very explicit and is printed *in extenso* in Mackenzie's History. The paragraph referring to Burns is in these terms: "The Right Worshipful Master having observed that Brother Burns was at present in the Lodge, who is well known as a great Poetic Writer, and for a late publication of his works, which have been universally commended, and submitted that he should be assumed a member of this Lodge, which was unanimously agreed to, and he was assumed accordingly." Thus he became an Honorary member of the Lodge. The History proceeds on the following page to relate that at the last monthly meeting of the season, held on 1 March, the Master conferred upon Burns "the title of Poet Laureate of the Lodge".

This statement of an obviously unconstitutional procedure has engendered perennial discussion in Masonic circles, fostered by its annual repetition in the Installation programme of the Lodge, probably in the expectation that by continued reiteration its authenticity may be eventually regarded as established. The topic has bulked so largely in Masonic annals and in books and papers on Burns, as to have become in certain quarters the preponderant feature of Burns's sojourn in Edinburgh. The cause of this notoriety was the painting of a picture by Stewart Watson in 1845, purporting to represent the scene of the Inauguration of Burns as Poet Laureate of Lodge Canongate Kilwinning, prints of which have been broadcast throughout the world; and the concurrent issue of Marshall's volume already mentioned, *A Winter with Robert Burns,* which gave biographical details of the personages depicted. These personages include some who were not members of the Order; one who did not set foot in Scotland until two years later; one who had left the country six years previously; and one who, never known to be a Freemason, was in his 108th year in 1787. It is noteworthy that the minute of this March meeting is not reproduced or quoted in Mackenzie's History and for a very excellent reason. This minute is also very explicit, much too explicit for satisfactory argument although argument there has been in abundance. It runs thus: "St John's Chapel, 1 March 1787. The Lodge being duly constituted, it was reported that since last meeting H. Dalrymple, Esq. (then follows a list of names) who all paid their dues to the Treasurer. No other business being before the meeting the Lodge adjourned." No mention is made of any election or inauguration of Burns, who as an Honorary member was not indeed eligible for office, nor of the institution of the new office of Poet Laureate; and two such remarkable items of *business* could not have escaped record if they had ever happened. But there was definitely *no other* business. There is no mention of such an important meeting in Grand Lodge records; no registration of such a distinguished office-bearer, and Grand Secretary Laurie, who published his *History of Freemasonry in Scotland* in 1804, makes no reference to an incident with which he must have been acquainted personally had it occurred. No items for the increased expenditure necessarily incurred in such a gathering appear in the Lodge accounts or elsewhere. Nor is there record of annual re-election as with other office bearers of the Lodge, and the Lodge had officially no Laureate for many years after Burns' day. The first mention of Burns in that capacity or of the office of Laureate occurs in the minute of 9 February 1815, when "the RW Master stated that he had observed a public subscription had been commenced for the purpose of erecting a Mausoleum to the Memory of Robert Burns, who was a member and Poet Laureate of this Lodge."

In another record, *The Book of Robert Burns,* by Dr Charles Rogers, the date of this presumed inauguration is given as 25 June. This is demonstrably untenable as Burns on that date was on his West Highland tour and wrote to Robert Ainslie on the 28th from Arrochar after travelling from Inveraray.

It is inconceivable that Burns himself would be silent over such an honour. In March 1787, he wrote to his friend, Mrs Dunlop, "The appellation of a Scottish bard is by far my highest pride." With such a pride the honour of a Laureateship in Edinburgh from the leaders of society would undoubtedly have evoked some record. Yet in none of his multitude of letters, nor in his Commonplace Book or Diary which he states he made his confidant, does he ever refer to the subject or even to Lodge Canongate Kilwinning.

The controversy had an important development in 1878 when D. Murray Lyon was about to publish his *History of Freemasonry in Scotland.* Following up some information he had received, the Secretary of Lodge Canongate Kilwinning "felt it to be his duty" to request from the author an assurance that in his forthcoming work any references to Burns' connection with that Lodge would not discredit that connection. A lengthy correspondence ensued – lengthy at least on the side of the Secretary – and Mackenzie in his History devotes no less than a dozen pages to it. But we find what D. Murray Lyon cynically describes as that same "tendency to represent the traditions of the Craft as historical facts or so to embellish facts as to distort if not altogether to obliterate them". The arguments advanced by the Secretary are mere sophistry, the main line being that as statements which had been widely circulated had never been contradicted they must be assumed to be correct. No more absurd assumption could be imagined. The arguments adduced would never be accepted by any judicature and were amply refuted at a later investigation. D. Murray Lyon's conclusions were: "When Marshall first made the assertion to a committee of the Lodge its records bear that his statement created surprise. There are many other facts which all go to show that the Poet's election and inauguration as Poet Laureate of this Lodge is a myth."

The matter was not allowed to end there. There was a lengthy correspondence in the Masonic press and on 29 December 1892, D. Murray Lyon, who had become Grand Secretary of the Grand Lodge of Scotland, drew the attention of Grand Committee to the inscription under the picture by Stewart Watson which was then on the wall of the Committee Room, having been presented to Grand Lodge in 1863 by the family of the late Sir James Burnes, Physician to the Army in Bombay. Grand Committee thereupon appointed a Special Committee consisting of Brothers William Officer, David Sneddon and Allan Mackenzie to "consider and report on the whole question". There was a long and critical enquiry followed by a detailed report which discredited not only the evidence advanced and the witnesses who supplied it, but also the picture and Marshall's volume. The witness, W. N. Fraser, for example, a Past Master of the Lodge, made the statement that "the honour was fully appreciated by the Bard. He alludes to the circumstances in the following lines:

> To please you, and praise you.
> Ye ken your Laureate scorns;
> The prayer still – you share still
> Of grateful minstrel Burns."

Yet we know that these lines were sent to Gavin Hamilton on 3 May 1786, before Burns had thought of a visit to Edinburgh. Campbell, who averred that he had spent two happy days with Burns at Auchtertyre Castle, was born in 1776, according to the official register, and was therefore in his eleventh year when Burns was at Auchtertyre and did not join the Craft till 5 February 1801. Yet he said that he "had had many opportunities of giving testimony in favour of the particulars referred to". The following were the conclusions of the Special Committee: "The Sub-Committee has bestowed much time and consideration on the matter remitted to it and enquired into it very fully. It regrets having to report:

1st. That in its opinion the statements made in *A Winter with Robert Burns* as to the creation of, election to, and inauguration of the Poet as Poet Laureate of the Lodge Canongate Kilwinning is fictitious;

2nd. That the office was not created during the lifetime of Burns and that consequently he was not elected to and was not inaugurated into it;

3rd. That the statement that Burns had been Poet Laureate of the Lodge Canongate Kilwinning was first made by the publisher of an engraving of Burns in October 1798; and

4th. That the statement that he had been inaugurated into that office was first made in November 1845, by the author of *A Winter with Robert Burns* and the painter of the picture representing the alleged inauguration."

This report was signed by William Officer and D. Sneddon; Mackenzie dissented, giving his reasons. But the inscription remains, with the picture, today.

The Edinburgh edition of Burns' poems was published on 21 April 1787, by Wm. Creech, the foremost publisher of the day and a member of Lodge Canongate Kilwinning. The printer was Wm. Smellie, also a member of the Craft and mainspring of the Crochallan Club. For the frontispiece Alexander Nasmyth, another member of Canongate Kilwinning and an artist of note, gratuitously painted the most reliable portrait of Burns from special sittings, and this was engraved for the volume by another member, John Beugo. These and other members of the Fraternity were the associates of Burns during this period, meeting not in lodges but in the popular taverns of the day such as John Dowie's in Liberton's Wynd or

Dannie Douglas's Howff in Anchor Close. Hence the success of this second, as of the first, edition may be credited to Masonic influence.

Delays in reaching a financial settlement with the dilatory Creech kept Burns in the city much beyond his original intention. This was unfortunate because it was disconcerting to his muse and afforded time and opportunity for other matters than the contemplation of his future vocation. These do not concern us here. That he had no misgiving as to the temporary nature of his residence in Edinburgh is evident from his letters. To Dr Moore on 23 April, he wrote, "I leave Edinburgh in the course of ten days or a fortnight and after a few pilgrimages over some of the classic ground of Caledonia, I shall return to my rural shades in all likelihood never more to quit them." He set out on the first of these pilgrimages on 5 May, with Robert Ainslie, a member of Lodge St Luke, now No. 44, and toured the Border country. At Eyemouth they became Royal Arch Masons, Ainslie paying a guinea while Burns, "on account of his remarkable poetic genius" was admitted without fee. In his diary of the tour, under date 19 May 1787, he notes "Spent the day at Mr Grieve's – made a Royal Arch Mason at Lodge St Abb (Eyemouth)." He returned to Edinburgh on 7 August, but Creech was still dawdling and Burns set about arranging for his longest tour. On 23 August he wrote to the "Men and Brethren" of Lodge St James: "I am truly sorry it is not in my power to be at your quarterly meeting. If I must be absent in body believe me I shall be present in spirit," and he repeated a stanza of his former song:

> "Within your dear mansion may wayward Contention
> Or withered Envy ne'er enter;
> May Secrecy round be the mystical bound,
> And brotherly Love be the centre."

He set off on his Highland tour two days later with Willie Nicol. They visited Linlithgow and Stirling in each of which towns Burns is said to have attended a local Lodge. But here again the reports are but legendary. They were not recorded in any minutes nor are they mentioned in letters or Diary as they would have been if true. He returned to Edinburgh on 16 September.

This second winter which he was fated to spend in Edinburgh against all his inclinations had not the glamour of the first. The novelty had worn off both on the part of Burns and some of his former friends and he was worried by Creech's continued failure to settle accounts. Freemasonry never came into the picture; an accident kept him for a great part of the time indoors. He left Edinburgh in the middle of February 1788, after a temporary financial arrangement with Creech and returned home. There was a bitter taste in his mouth, evidenced by his feelings when he wrote of "the world of wits and *gens comme il faut* which I lately left and with whom I never again will intimately mix."

The Edinburgh periods in the career of Burns here touched upon were short but as already indicated were fateful, and beyond providing the original friendships which made them memorable Freemasonry as such had no direct part. They were fateful for several reasons. They gave to the world at large the poems and in great measure the revealing letters of Burns. They afforded the opportunity for the display and the preservation for posterity of his supreme gift of song, by his association with James Johnson and the collaborating musician, Stephen Clark, in *The*

Scots Musical Museum. They introduced Burns to a new profession which was his stand-by in later years. And they led him into two branches of social life, the drawing room and the city tavern, which even on his own admission had fateful consequences; they "ate up slices of his constitution".

Another great poet has told us that there is a tide in the affairs of men which taken at the flood leads on to fortune. Burns did not reach that haven. Did he fail to take the tide at the flood or did the flood come too late, if indeed it ever came during his lifetime. Who can or dare venture to say? During the ages of this world many men have passed of whom it may with truth be said, "He being dead yet speaketh." High up on that list is Robert Burns.

EDITOR'S FOOTNOTES TO CHAPTER EIGHT

1 Having by arrangement stayed overnight at Covington Mains in the parish of Thankerton, near Biggar.
2. Brother James Dalrymple was a member of Lodge St James, No. 135 and later its Master.
3. Francis Charteris, Lord Elcho, later 7th Earl of Wemyss.

Chapter Nine

ROBERT BURNS AND LODGE CANONGATE KILWINNING

By Brother Lt Cdr D. Currie, PM, Lodge Canongate Kilwinning, No. 2.

At a meeting of Lodge Canongate Kilwinning in 1816 the Master called the attention of the members to a paper he was holding. This was, he said, a copy of a subscription list to a mausoleum to be erected at Dumfries in the memory of the poet, Robert Burns, who, said the Master, was "LATELY POET LAUREATE OF THIS LODGE". That occasion was the first time that the name of Burns was mentioned in the minutes of the Lodge in conjunction with the office of Poet Laureate, and from that meeting onwards the Laureateship has been the subject of discussion which at times has been acrimonious and bitter. More than once it has been the subject of fiery debate on the floor of Grand Lodge. During the latter part of the nineteenth century the reputation of the Grand Secretary, Brother David Murray Lyon, came under some risk and it was decided to appoint a Special Sub-committee of Grand Committee to decide once and for all whether Burns had ever been Poet Laureate of the Lodge. The Sub-committee reported that it could find no grounds to support the contention that Burns had been installed as Poet Laureate.

Many Freemasons of renown have studied the subject, and have stated their opinions on the matter, among them being Brother Alan Mackenzie, a Past Master of Lodge Canongate and the author during the last century of the Lodge History. He was a member of Grand Committee and of the Special Sub-committee, and he published a minority report showing where the Sub-committee report was in error.

In raising again a subject which has engendered such passions in the past one has to exercise great care. The facts have to be examined and if it is possible any new material has to be considered. We have to seek out any parallel situations which might assist in reaching a conclusion.

In considering the facts it is necessary to separate written records from recollections and in this case the written records can soon be disposed of:

(a) The minutes of Lodge Canongate indicate that Burns attended on one occasion only, which was the meeting on 1 February 1787.

(b) The minute of that meeting includes the following passage: "The R.W.M., having observed that Brother Burns was at present in the Lodge, who is well known as a great Poetic Writer, and for a late publication of his works, which have been universally commended, and submitted that he should be assumed to be a member of this Lodge, which was unanimously agreed to, and he was assumed accordingly."

(c) The next mention of Burns in the minutes was that of 1816, when the Master referred to him as "Lately Poet Laureate of this Lodge".

In 1846, Brother Stewart Watson, the artist, who had been Secretary of the Lodge, produced his painting (now in the museum of Grand Lodge) of the Inauguration of Burns as Poet Laureate on 1 March 1787. At the same time, another member of the Lodge produced a book *A Winter with Robert Burns* which, apart from other content, gave biographical note on the men shown in the painting. The author was Brother John Marshall.

At various times, members of the Lodge claimed to have been present at the Inauguration, but no claim of that nature was made during the first ten years following the poet's demise Two Brethren in particular made this claim – Brothers Charles Moore and William Petrie. Moore was a banker who had held office in the Lodge, but he was a very old man before he first made the claim. Petrie was the Lodge Tyler and as such was a paid servant of the Lodge who was not within the Chapel at meetings.

As far as the minutes of the Lodge are concerned it is obvious that there is not one word to support the assertion that Burns was Inaugurated as Poet Laureate. Stewart Watson's painting, whilst carrying great merit as a work of art, was a commercial production and, as there was no record of the Inauguration, it cannot be considered as providing evidence. In fact, some of the characters shown as being present had died before 1787, and others were never members of the Craft. The criticism levelled at the painting applies equally to Marshall's book.

What about parallel situations? Almost contemporary with Burns was Admiral Lord Nelson, following whose death at Trafalgar in 1805 memorials were erected in two Lodges in England to the memory of "our dear Brother, Nelson of Bronte". Nelson was certainly not a Freemason, nor was he the only example of a Mason being made posthumously. It would appear to be logical that if a man could be made a Mason after his death, then a Mason could be made an Office-bearer posthumously. It is certainly within the bounds of possibility that the Master in 1816, when referred to Burns as "lately Poet Laureate of the Lodge" was aware of the Nelsonic example and was giving the Lodge a posthumous Office-bearer.

Burns himself, when asked for memories of his visit to Edinburgh, never referred to having been inaugurated as Poet Laureate. He referred to an incident which had occurred when he visited the Lodge Edinburgh St Andrew. Burns was a visitor, as was the Grand Master Mason, Francis Charteris, and to the poet's surprise the Grand Master toasted "Caledonia and Caledonia's Bard – Robert Burns".

My own view, after studying the evidence, is that if Burns was the Poet Laureate then his appointment resulted from the Master's statement in 1816, a conclusion which I reached some years ago. Earlier this year (1993) I learned that around the year 1800 a minister of the Church of Scotland, Rev John Macdonald, was appointed to a living at Anstruther, in Fife. He had previously been employed as a private tutor in Perth, a position which he resigned in 1796 in order to travel around Scotland. He had kept a diary, or journal, of his wanderings, and his manuscript is now held in the archives of the University of St Andrews. Rev Macdonald states that he was in Dumfries some weeks before Burns' death, and was honoured to dine privately with the bard one evening. During the course of a pleasant meal the poet entertained him with a description of the evening he was made Poet Laureate to a group of Jacobite gentlemen in Edinburgh. Robert Burns never made any secret of his Freemasonry and it would be out of character for him to try to hide a connection with a Masonic group by giving them another name. There is, however, the possibility that some of the group were members of Lodge Canongate, and that with the passage of time they became confused between groups.

Part Three

Chapter Ten

ELLISLAND

Having settled with Creech, his publisher, in February 1788 Burns found himself master of nearly £500 after discharging all his expenses. There would appear to be some discrepancy regarding the emoluments he received from the publishing of his first "Edinburgh edition". Nicol, his close friend, claimed Burns had received £600 for the edition and a further £100 for the copyright. Dr Currie claimed the gross product of Creech's edition was £500. In one of his letters Burns stated a figure of £400.

Be that as it may, he immediately advanced £200 to Brother Gilbert who had undertaken the support of their mother. With the remainder he determined to settle himself for life in farming and took from Mr Miller, Dalswinton, the farm of Ellisland, some six miles north of Dumfries, which he entered at Whitsun 1788. Burns took up residence alone as the house required considerable refurbishment. He immediately engaged in rebuilding the dwelling house which in the state he found it was totally inadequate to the accommodation of his family.

While the house was building Burns occupied what he termed "an old smoking spence" on its outskirts while Jean, with whom he had recently joined in a public declaration of marriage, remained in Mauchline.

Towards the end of the year the family joined him at Ellisland. During the three and a half years Burns was at Ellisland it could be said that his active participation in Masonry was limited. Ever the ardent Freemason he had, on 12 December 1788, affiliated to Lodge St Andrew, No. 179 Dumfries and he retained his connection with this Lodge to the end. Indeed it became known as "Burns' Lodge". His affiliation fee was ten shillings.

The Minute which records his admission is a quaint one and full of inaccuracies both as to spelling and figures:

"The Brethren having celebrated the Anniversary of St John in the usual manner and Brother Burns in Ellisland of St Davids Strabolton Lodge, No. 178 being present the Lodge unanimously assumed him a member of the Lodge being a Master Mason be subscribed the regulations as a member thereafter the Lodge was shut.
Signed Sim Mackenzie."

The next mention of the poet is made in the Minute of 28 December 1789, when his name appears on the list of those present and as having made payment, along with the other members, of his quarterly fees. Then again he is one of five Brethren who met in the Globe Tavern, Dumfries in April 1790, when, as usual, friendships were established, one of his friends presenting him with an apron of "Chamois leather, very fine, with figures of gold, some of them relieved with green, others with a dark red colour (while) on the under side of the semi-circular part which is turned down at the top is written in a bold, fair hand: Charles Sharpe, of Hotham, to Rabbie Burns, Dumfries, Dec. 12 1791". Burns and Sharpe were mutually interested in music and verse.

Though his attendances at Lodge meetings during this period were few the reasons are not hard to seek:

1. Initially the rebuilding etc. of the farmhouse etc. must have been time consuming.
2. His application to the labours on the farm were interrupted by visits to his wife and family still in Ayrshire and as the distance was too great for a single day's journey he generally spent the night at an Inn on the way – e.g. at Sanquhar or New Cumnock (remember the incident which produced the Ode, Sacred to the Memory of Mrs Oswald).
3. His fame naturally attracted the attention of neighbours and he found himself the welcome guest at the festive board of farming neighbours and also at Millers of Dalswinton, the Riddells of Friars Carse etc.
4. Finding time for the laudable work of founding and furnishing and at times sharing in the management of a parish library at Dunscore.
5. Undertaking a considerable volume of literary writings – letters, poems, songs etc. – especially songs for Johnson.
6. Through the good offices of his friend, Mr Graham, his application for a post with the Excise was granted and he was appointed to perform his duties of gauger over some ten parishes around Ellisland – an appointment which found him riding some 200 miles a week.
7. His renowned social and poetic gifts brought him a good deal of distraction in the form of visitors at Ellisland. Nor was that all. During this hectic time at Ellisland, Burns found time to write some of his best and most revealing letters – the majority to Mrs Dunlop – and a substantial body of verse e.g. Tam O'Shanter, The Whistle, Epistle to Dr Blacklock, To the Toothache, To Mary in Heaven, Of a' the Airts, Auld Lang Syne, John Anderson my Jo, Ca' the Yowes, Ye Banks and Braes o'Bonnie Doon, Ae fond Kiss, to mention but a few.

In addition here at Ellisland he began what has become known as the Glenriddell Manuscript into which he copied a selection of what he considered to be his best letters.

All of these activities, in time, understandably interfered with the attention Burns could give to his farm and contributed to the abstraction of his thoughts from the business of agriculture.

Although the rent for Ellisland was both moderate and reasonable Burns, not surprisingly, found it convenient if not necessary to resign his farm and move into Dumfries.

Chapter Eleven

LATER LIFE AND HIS LAST DAYS

In November 1791, Burns moved into Dumfries, a bustling, pleasant, lively town of some 5,600 inhabitants. Here he soon made many new friends both from ordinary folk he met in the Globe Tavern but also among professional people who appreciated the brilliance of his intellectual powers – e.g. Dr Maxwell, John Syme, James Gray, Alexander Findlater etc.

He was most assiduous in carrying out his Excise duties. He patronised the theatre and contributed several Prologues to be delivered by well-known actors and actresses. He wrote industriously for Thomson's Collection while continuing to write for Johnson. Indeed he provided about 160 songs for Johnson and some 114 for Thomson. In the main this was a time of artistic enrichment and fulfilment. In addition he made several excursions, accompanied by his friend Syme, through some of the most picturesque and romantic areas of the neighbouring countryside. An interesting account of one of these journeys has been preserved for us in a well-recorded letter from Syme to Dr Currie, Burns' first biographer.

Also, no longer having to face the tedious round trip of 12 miles from Ellisland to Dumfries his attendances at Lodge St Andrew were more frequent.

On 27 December 1791 and on 6 February and 14 May 1792, he was again present at meetings of the Lodge when he acted as Steward. On 31 May of that year he took part in the proceedings, part of which was ordering the clerk to procure "a proper silver seal for the use of the Lodge". On 5 June he appears again. He attended on 22 and 30 November of that year, and at the latter meeting (St Andrew's Day), was elected to the Senior Warden's chair, which office he filled for a year. Exactly a year later "The Senior Warden" (Burns) is noted as being present. His name does not appear again until 29 November 1794, when the election of office-bearers took place, and over a year elapses before his name is mentioned on the sederunt, when on 28 January 1796 he stood sponsor for a candidate "a merchant in Liverpool who, being recommended by Burns, was admitted apprentice". At this meeting the Brethren agreed that the new Apprentice's "fees be applied towards defraying the expenses of this night". While a member of Lodge St Andrew, out of a possible sixteen meetings he was present at eleven of them. His final attendance was on 14 April 1796, out of loyalty to Capt Adam Gordon, who was initiated on that occasion.

In the main these were indeed happy days when for long stretches at a time, as he himself put it, he was "in song".

Not withstanding the elation, clouds had darkened his horizon:-

1. His expressed sympathy for the French Revolution.
2. The "4 carronades" incident.
3. The "Ca Ira" incident at the gala performance of "As you like it" in the local theatre.
4. His alleged failure to rise to his feet when the National Anthem was played.

Eyebrows were being raised and tongues had begun to wag. Murmurs of disquiet and allegations of disloyalty to the Crown and disaffection to the government were putting his Excise appointment at risk. He defended himself in a spirited letter to Mr Graham which, *inter alia*, contains this interesting paragraph:

"I never uttered any invective against the King – his private worth, it is altogether impossible that such a man as I, can appreciate, and in his private capacity, I always revered and ever will, with the soundest loyalty, revere, the monarch of Great Britain as, to speak in Masonic, the sacred Keystone of our Royal Arch Constitution."

His position was secure but prospects of advancement may have been greatly put at risk. But a more ominous cloud on the horizon was beginning to give cause for concern – *viz.* growing anxiety regarding his health.

In 1789 while at Ellisland he was ill with, what he termed as "malignant squinary slow fever". In a letter to Mrs Dunlop in June 1794 he had stated that for some time he had been in poor health and threatened with "flying gout". In a letter to Maria Riddell dated "Spring 1795" he tells her that he is "so ill as to be scarce able to hold this miserable pen to this miserable paper".

In the autumn of 1795 his health, never very sound, finally broke down but he struggled on attending to his official duties and all the time growing weaker and weaker. In September 1795 he lost a dearly-loved daughter, three years of age, who had been sent to Mauchline for reasons of health, and his bitter anguish was intensified by the fact that owing to his own serious illness he could not be present at her funeral. For by this time the deadly malady from which he had suffered for twenty years, and which in the light of modern medical research has been ably and fully explained by Sir James Crichton Browne, had begun to sap his remaining strength. During December-January 1795/96 he was ill with rheumatic fever. Dr Maxwell prescribed sea-bathing in country quarters and horse-riding for the remainder of the summer. On 3 July he went to Brow, on the Solway, a small village with a reputation as a Spa. The change did not benefit him. On Monday 18 July 1796 he arrived back in Dumfries, in a borrowed gig. That same day he wrote his last letter – to his father-in-law in Mauchline. The news that the Poet was dying soon spread and outside in the streets anxious groups of townsfolk gathered, eager to know the latest news. They had not long to wait. On 21 July Burns was dead.

Of the poet's funeral Dr Currie has given a full account. We quote at length:

The death of Burns made a strong and general impression on all who had interested themselves in his character, and especially on the inhabitants of the town and county in which he had spent the latter years of his life. Flagrant as his follies and errors had been, they had not deprived him of the respect and regard entertained for the extraordinary powers of his genius, and the generous qualities of his heart. The Gentlemen Volunteers of Dumfries determined to bury their illustrious associate with military honours, and every preparation was made to render this last service solemn and impressive. The Fencible Infantry of Angus-shire, and the regiment of cavalry of the Cinque Ports, at that time quartered in Dumfries, offered their assistance on this occasion; the principal inhabitants of the town and neighbourhood determined to walk in the funeral procession; and a vast concourse of persons assembled, some of them from considerable distance, to witness the obsequies of the Scottish Bard. On the evening of 24 July, the remains of Burns were removed from his house to the Town Hall, and the funeral took place on the succeeding day. A party of the volunteers, selected to perform the military duty in the churchyard, stationed themselves in the front of the procession, with their arms reversed; the main body of the corps surrounded and supported the coffin, on which were placed the hat and sword of their friend and fellow soldier; the numerous body of attendants ranged themselves in the rear; while the Fencible regiments of infantry and cavalry lined the streets from the Town Hall to the burial ground in the southern churchyard, a distance of more than half a mile. The whole procession moved forward to that sublime and affecting strain of music, the "Dead March in Saul"; and three volleys fired over his grave marked the return of Burns to his parent earth! The spectacle was in a high degree grand and solemn, and accorded with the general sentiments of sympathy and sorrow which the occasion had called forth.

The remains of Burns were originally interred in a small enclosure at the north corner of St Michael's churchyard at Dumfries; in the same grave, two of his children were afterwards buried. The spot continued for many years to be undistinguished by any memorial of public feeling. It was covered only by a plain slab, which his widow, under the influence of a less inconstant sentiment, had procured from her slender funds, and caused to be inscribed in the following terms, touching by their unambitious simplicity:

> "In memory of Robert Burns, who died on the 21st July 1796, in the 38th year of his age; and Maxwell Burns, who died on the 25th April 1799, aged 2 years and 9 months: also of Francis Wallace Burns, who died on the 9th July 1803, aged 14 years."

The erection of a public monument or mausoleum at Dumfries was not seriously contemplated till the year 1814, when on 6 January a meeting took place in that town and it was determined by those present that "a mausoleum ought to be reared over the grave of Burns". A committee was at the same time formed, including noblemen, gentlemen, clergymen and some of the principal citizens of Dumfries, for the purpose of collecting subscriptions and superintending the erection of the proposed building. Money being liberally forwarded, not only from the various provinces of Scotland but from other parts of the United Kingdom, from the East and West Indies and from America, the committee were soon enabled to proceed to the more interesting part of their duty. A plan by Brother Thomas Frederick Hunt of London, having been selected from those furnished by various competing architects, the foundation stone was laid by a masonic procession, on 5 June 1815, William Miller, Esq, of Dalswinton superintending the ceremony. The situation chosen for the building was different from that in which the remains of Burns had been laid. That spot being low and confined in an angle of the churchyard it was found necessary to assume a situation near the east corner, where accordingly the building has been erected, the form adopted being that of a plain Doric temple reared about a sepulchral vault. When the latter had been completed the remains of the Poet and of his two deceased children were raised from their original resting place and transferred thither (9 September) with as much privacy and as much delicacy as the circumstances of the case rendered possible. The building was completed in 1817, the whole expense being about £1,500.

The Future of Lodge St Andrew

The Lodge ceased to meet in 1805, and an attempt was made in 1815 to revive it, when the Minute closes with a resolution to support the Provincial Grand Master, now William Millar of Dalswinton, at laying the foundation stone (on 5 June) of the Mausoleum to be erected over the remains of Robert Burns, the most distinguished Brother that Lodge St Andrew had been privileged to receive within its portals. Several Lodges attended the ceremony, but St Andrew is not mentioned as being represented, although over 400 Freemasons took part in the proceedings. Efforts to revive it proved futile and no other meetings are recorded. It was struck off the roll of the Grand Lodge of Scotland in 1816. No reference is made in any of the other Lodges, meeting regularly while Burns lived in Dumfries, to his having paid them any visits, though no doubt he took his share of their proceedings from time to time, and thus it is to the precious Minute Book of the Lodge alone that we are indebted for some knowledge of the Masonic activities of our national poet during his stay in Dumfries.

In December 1879, at a public sale, certain articles, once the property of Lodge St Andrew, No. 179, were purchased and paid for by the then Grand Master Mason, Sir Michael Shaw Stewart, Baronet, who presented them to the Grand Lodge of Scotland. These were – (1) The Minute Book of Lodge St Andrew, Dumfries, No. 179, of which Burns was an affiliated member, bearing the poet's signature to the Bye-laws and containing the Minute of his admission; (2) the mallet of St Andrew's, and (3) an apron used in the Lodge in Burns' time. These are on exhibit in the Grand Lodge Museum.

In the British Museum is an item of interest to all concerned with Robert Burns – his famous punch bowl. It was given to him by James Armour as a wedding present when he at last married his daughter, Jean. The union was officially recognised by the Mauchline Kirk Session on 5 August 1788. As Robert fought to make a home for her at Ellisland he wrote:

> Of a' the airts the wind can blaw,
>   I dearly like the west,
> For there the bonnie lassie lives,
>   The lassie I lo'e best:
> There wild woods grow, and rivers row
>   And mony a hill between;
> But day and night my fancy's flight
>   Is ever wi' my Jean.
>
>   [airts = directions]

The bowl of Inverary marble was a natural present for James Armour to give for he was by trade a stone-mason and could easily have made it. There is no doubt that Burns put it to good use. Dr Currie wrote of one occasion in *The Works of Burns* (1800), vol. 1: "he produced at the same time his punch bowl, made of Inverary marble, and, mixing the spirit with water and sugar filled their glasses, and invited them to drink".

After Robert's death in 1796 his widow directed that the bowl should be sent to Alexander Cunningham in Edinburgh. This was done by his brother Gilbert with a letter:

Dumfries, 16th January 1801

Dear Sir,
I herewith send you a small punch-bowl in Inverary marble. To present you with so paltry a vessel of such base material requires some explanation. Mrs Burns has for some time expressed a wish to present you with some small testimony of the sense she has of your friendly attachment to her children as well as to their father. I have advised her that as this bowl has acquired some celebrity from Dr Currie's having connected it with his descrip-

tion of the social powers as well as habits of its former owner, it will be an agreeable present to you, and I hope it will reach you while Mr Syme is with you, that in his company the melancholy luxury of the recollection of joys that are past may be produced in your mind so susceptible of tender impressions.

> I am, Dear Sir,
> Yours most truly,
> Gilbert Burns.

The Burns Bowl, now in the British Museum

Cunningham must have been pleased to have this present, for he immediately had silver mounts made for the rim and for the foot of the bowl. On that which surrounds the rim is engraved an appropriate quotation from a Burns poem:

> But ye whom social pleasure charms,
> Whose hearts the tide of kindness warms,
> Who hold your being on the terms
> "Each aid the others"
> Come to my Bowl, come to my arms,
> My FRIENDS, my BROTHERS!

Cunningham died on 27 January 1812 and there is no evidence of what happened to the bowl while it was in his possession. In the Edinburgh Press some four years later, however, an auction sale was advertised to take place on Saturday, 21 January 1816. Ballantyne, the auctioneer, records in his diary that the sale raised some five hundred pounds and that the bowl was sold for eighty-four pounds.

The bowl next appeared in London where it was apparently in use at a tavern in the Strand owned by a man named Cochran. It is fortunate that Cochran pawned the bowl and sold the ticket to Archibald Hastie who immediately redeemed the pledged item for the sum of forty pounds. This occurred in about the year 1830 and in April 1858 the Trustees of the British Museum were pleased to accept the Burns bowl into their safe keeping at the bequest of Mr Hastie. It has remained in their keeping ever since and is on display.

After the death of the poet on 21 July 1796 his body lay in state at the Town Hall until 26 July. The funeral took place on a fine day, the local Volunteers according full military honours. Some thousands of people were present at the interment in a quiet corner of St Michael's churchyard and on the grave was placed a plain tomb-stone bearing simply the name and age of the poet. A public subscription was launched in 1813, raising a large sum of money which enabled a mausoleum to be built on an elevated site in the churchyard. The remains of Robert Burns were transferred to it with solemn dignity on 19 September 1815.

Part Four

This section comprises three Treatises relating to the Masonic writings of Robert Burns.

There is, of necessity, considerable duplication of material but no apology is offered on this account as each lecture contains a certain amount of biographical detail and each quotation is to be considered within this context.

    1. Robert Burns Poet and Freemason
    2. The Masonic Genius of Robert Burns
    3. Robert Burns as a Freemason

Chapter Twelve

Lecture One

ROBERT BURNS, POET AND FREEMASON

By Brother John Webb

The 18th century can rightly be claimed as a period of climax in Scottish history. As early as in 1707, the Act of Union received the Royal Assent and from the first day of May in the year 1707 and "for ever after" Scotland and England would be united. Article three of that Act determined "that the United Kingdom be represented by one Parliament". By 1783 this position had become generally approved and Scotland returned its own representatives to Parliament in London.

Further dramatic changes also occurred in Scotland, these being mainly due to the Highland risings of 1715 and 1745. The end of Jacobitism and the clan system made possible the reconciliation of the Highlands and Lowlands and their fusion into a single Scottish nation. The agrarian revolution spread to the Highlands and changes in the nature of farming became evident among the largest landowners. Religious bigotry declined and rigid Calvinism was replaced by a more moderate and temperate approach.

In a century of political unrest, not only in Scotland but in Europe also, man began to search for dignity and for self expression. At the end of the century France found a solution in bloody revolution. It says much for the cool nature and clear thinking of the people of Scotland that the desire for change was channelled into proper and governable bounds. They looked for something which could bind them together in a fellowship which would strengthen national bonds. It was a convivial age and in many ways the 18th century was strangely adapted to enable the root of Freemasonry to be nurtured and developed. The need to meet fraternal friendship and to strengthen natural relationships was met by the foundation of lodges. The after-proceedings were also part of the social progress and development within communities. Freemasonry offered the opportunity for men from various backgrounds to meet as brethren. In the middle of the century, on 25 January 1759, Robert Burns was born at Alloway near Ayr in Scotland, close to the "Auld Brig o' Doon".

His father, William Burness or Burnes, was the son of a farmer in Kincardineshire. The farm became forfeit in consequence of the Rebellion of 1715 in which the noble house of Keith Marischall took part. William Burness left the family home at the age of 19 to settle in the west of Scotland. After labouring near Edinburgh for a number of years he eventually found his way towards Ayrshire. He became a gardener and overseer to a Mr Ferguson of Doonholm and in December 1757 he married Agnes Brown. Robert was the first-born child of their marriage.

The Early Years

Other children followed: Gilbert (1760-1832), Agnes (1762-1834), Annabella (1764-1832), William (1767-90), John (1769-85), and Isabella (1771-1858). At the Whitsuntide of 1766, when Robert was between six and seven years of age, William Burness removed from his Alloway home to a farm at Mount Oliphant, also in the parish of Ayr. This farm did not prosper, and some six years[1] later the roots of the family were again disturbed and William Burness became the tenant of a larger and somewhat better farm at Lochlea in the parish of Tarbolton.

Despite the worries of farming Burness did not neglect the education of his sons. At the age of six Robert was sent to a small school at Alloway Mill where for a short time he came under the influence of Mr Campbell. When Mr Campbell moved to another situation Burness and some of his neighbours engaged a Mr John Murdoch who would be paid by the parents and lodged in turn by them in their own homes. It was from Murdoch that a record survives of the devoted nature of William Burness towards his family and the strong influence he exerted in maintaining a high moral standard. Later in life Robert wrote one of the most famous of his poems which reflects very much the nature of his up-bringing namely "The Cotter's Saturday Night".

It becomes obvious from the studies made of this period of the poet's life, and from the records left by his brother Gilbert, that they both benefited greatly from Murdoch's tuition and later from the discussions which they had with their father whilst living at Mount Oliphant. They were encouraged to read widely and to study the Bible. Gilbert wrote of Robert at that time, "no book was so voluminous as to slacken his industry, or so antiquated as to dampen his researches". The family, however, were very poor, as the two sons have noted.

Robert wrote: "We lived very poorly. I was a dextrous ploughman for my age; and the next eldest to me was a brother (Gilbert), who could drive the plough very well and help me to thresh the corn." Of the same period Gilbert later wrote: "To the buffetings of misfortune we could only oppose hard labour and the most rigid economy. My brother, at the age of thirteen, assisted in thrashing the crop of corn, and at fifteen was the principal labourer on the farm, for we had no hired help." Despite these difficulties Robert Burns continued with his education, for in this period he assisted his tutor Murdoch with a revision of an English Grammar and took a course in French at which he became very proficient. He was further encouraged to learn Latin and to widen his selection of reading.

With the farm at Mount Oliphant failing, and when Robert was eighteen years of age, they moved to Lochlea where for a while they appeared to prosper. Robert by now had produced some poems and songs. He pledges his inspiration at the time to "a bonnie, sweet, sonsie lass", and says: "Thus began with me love and poetry; which at times have been my only, and till within the last twelve months, have been my highest enjoyment." Shortly before moving to Lochlea, Robert had been sent to Hugh Rodgers's School at Kirkoswald to learn mensuration, surveying, trigonometry and dialling. Whilst displaced from his home he became well informed in the knowledge of mankind. The contraband trade was then very successful and from time to time Burns joined with his companions who carried it on. He also learned to drink and from his own notes it is obvious that he learned to look after himself when engaged in a drunken squabble. In spite of all that he returned to his home considerably improved.

In 1779 Robert defied his father and joined a dancing class which was held in Tarbolton. Both Robert and Gilbert write of this period, and Robert remarks, "from that moment of disobedience in me he took a sort of dislike to me, which I believe was one cause of the dissipation which marked my succeeding years". The class took place in an upstairs room in John Richard's house, and in this same room, in 1780, the Bachelors' Club was founded in which Robert and Gilbert were leading members and debaters. The object of this club was to meet for discussion, mutual entertainment and improvement.

Freemasonry at Tarbolton

On 17 May 1771, the old and then independent Lodge of Kilwinning chartered a lodge, not surprisingly, named Tarbolton Kilwinning but internal troubles arose and early in 1773 twenty brethren, headed by Sir Thomas Wallace, Baronet, petitioned the Grand Lodge of Scotland who granted a warrant on 5 February for the Lodge of St David No. 174 (now No. 133). Among the signatures on that document was that of the Earl of Dumfries, the then Grand Master Mason.

The remaining members of Tarbolton Kilwinning, quick to appreciate the growing power of the Grand Lodge at Edinburgh, also sought a warrant therefrom and on 27 May 1774 they became Lodge St James Tarbolton Kilwinning No. 178. Before many years had passed, St David and St James decided to unite. The Minutes of St David record a proposal to that effect on 6 December 1780, and in the following June there appeared:

> . . . and having considered on our offers to Lodge St James respecting a junchen, also their answers, finds by a majority of votes that both may unite in terms offered and exchanged this day.

On 25 June the two lodges became one, as Lodge St David. The reason given for the choice of this name, "being the oldest charter" omitted mention of the Kilwinning Lodge of 1771!

Robert Burns is made a Mason

It was nine days after the amalgamation that Burns was admitted to Lodge St David No. 174. It being the only business of the meeting, the Minute is brief and to the point: "4 July 1781. Robert Burns in Lochly was entered an apprentice". His entry fee of twelve shillings and sixpence was paid on that day and the brother who performed the ceremony was Alexander Wood, a tailor of Tarbolton.[2]

Shortly after his initiation Burns left for Irvine, some twelve miles from his home in Lochlea. Of this move he recounts in his memoirs:

> I joined a flax dresser in Irvine to learn his trade. This was an unlucky affair, and to finish the whole, as we were giving a welcome carousal to the New Year, the shop took fire and burnt to ashes; and I was left like a true poet, not worth a sixpence.

During the time that he was thus displaced from Tarbolton he returned on 1 October 1781 for his second and third degrees, as the Minutes record:

Robert Burns in Lochly was passed and raised, Henry Cowan being Master, James Humphrey Senr. Warden and Alexr. Smith Junr. Do., Robert Wodrow Secy., and James Manson Treasurer and John Tannock Taylor and others of the Brethren being present. ("Taylor" is a misspelling for "Tyler".)

As to the three degree ceremonies there has been some disagreement as to where these took place. From the lodge records it became apparent that the only hall in Tarbolton at that time was the room used for the dancing class and by the Bachelors' Club. Since it was in a prominent public house run by John Richard, a Steward of the lodge, and Burns was already well known there, this was probably the room used. The mention of Manson's public house does not occur in the Minutes of the lodge until 1784. Of interest is the fact that the inn in which the Bachelors' club and the dancing classes were held is still to be seen in Tarbolton and in an excellent state of preservation.

Masonic Complications

It was at Lochlea on 13 February 1784 that William Burness died after a desperate struggle against poverty and the additional burdens of a court case in connection with the lease of the farm. It was this stroke of fate that caused Robert and Gilbert to attempt a joint venture at a new farm at Mossgiel a few miles further south. This was a family concern and was to last as such for four years. Robert was fortunate to have as a friend at that time a Mr Gavin Hamilton who was the agent for the Earl of Loudon, the owner of the farm and a member of the lodge. However, all was not well with Lodge St David. Wodrow and Manson, the Secretary and Treasurer, had been displeased by the choice of its new name rather than that of Lodge St James. They were joined by Robert Burns and Captain James Montgomerie in breaking away to reactivate Lodge St James whose charter had never been cancelled. It was to meet at Manson's inn. Despite an appeal to Grand Lodge by Lodge St David and proceedings at the Sheriff's Court at Ayr there was nothing that could be done. The Minute book of the Lodge St James records:

> Tarbolton 17 June 1782. St James's Lodge met upon the same footing as it was before the junction. James Montgomerie Gr. Mr. for the night.

Robert Burns' name does not appear again in the Minutes of either lodge until he was elected Depute Master of Lodge St James on 27 June 1784; it continued throughout Burns' active membership to meet at Manson's Inn.

St James's Minute book, which is carefully preserved, contains three entries actually written by Burns. The first of these is for 1 September 1784: "This night the lodge met and ordered four pounds of candles and one quire of eightpence paper for the use of the lodge, which money was laid out by the treasurer and the candles and paper laid in accordingly."

On twenty-nine occasions, between 29 June 1785 and 23 May 1788 Burns signed the Minutes as Depute Master. There are interesting differences in the signatures for, before 1 March 1786, we find "Robt. Burness": from that date, when his brother Gilbert was entered, passed and raised, Robert and Gilbert signed as "Burns".

23 June 1786. A minute of Lodge St James in Burns' handwriting

In one of many papers about Robert Burns it is noted that in his term as Depute Master the brethren were convened no less than seventy times and of these Burns was present on thirty-three occasions. It is recorded in the official history of the lodge that the lodge, or a deputation from it, met at Mauchline and on one occasion, 5 October 1786, the lodge met at Sorn with Burns in the chair. During this period certain distinguished persons were admitted to the lodge as honorary members. They included Professor Dugald Stewart of Catrine, Claude Alexander of Ballochmyle, Claude Neilson of Paisley, and Dr George Grierson of Glasgow. It was mainly due to the influence of Lodge St James that the Lodge of St Mungo was chartered in Mauchline in 1791.

Poet's Progress

The winter of 1785 to 1786 saw the emergence of Burns as a poet. As already mentioned, he had formed a great friendship with Gavin Hamilton, a lawyer and the agent of the Mossgiel Farm, and he it was who persuaded Burns to make a collection of his poems and to publish them. It was Hamilton who encouraged Burns to visit other lodges in Ayrshire and on 27 March 1786 Robert visited the Louden Kilwinning Lodge of which Hamilton was the Master. He was introduced into the lodge and became a member, Brother John Morton being responsible for his admission fee. It was to Gavin Hamilton that he dedicated a long poem which ends

> If friendless, low, we meet together,
> Then, Sir, your hand – my friend and brother!

Four years later, on the feast day of St John the Baptist, 24 June 1790, he wrote a reminder to Mr. John McKenzie that a meeting would take place:

> Friday first's the day appointed,
> By our Right Worshipful anointed,
> To hold our grand procession;
>   To get a blade o' Johnnie's morals,
>   And taste a swatch o' Manson's barrels,
>   I' the way of our profession.

Our Master and the Brotherhood
    Wad a' be glad to see you;
For me I would be mair than proud
    To share the mercies wi' you.
        If Death, then, wi' scaith, then,
            Some mortal heat is hechtin',
        Inform him, and storm him,
            That Saturday ye'll fecht him.

(blade = piece, specimen; swatch = sample; scath = hurt, damage, hechtin' = promising; storm = make a vigorous assault; fecht = fight.)

It is unfortunate that Burns's domestic affairs were not well attended to and the year 1786 saw him in desperate plight and planning emigration to Jamaica. He had formed an attachment to Jean Armour, the daughter of a master mason living in the village of Mauchline. Unfortunately for Burns, she was pregnant and, when the two met, Burns gave her a letter of acknowledgement of marriage which, by Scots law, was legal evidence that an irregular marriage had taken place. Jean's father received the information with anger and surprise. He influenced his daughter to reject Burns and to destroy the letter he had given her. In the course of time Jean became the mother of twins and Burns was summoned to provide for the children. In his poverty and with deeply wounded feelings of love and pride he saw the future as bleak and hopeless.

The alternative which attracted him was to leave his farm and to seek for himself a situation in Jamaica. With this in mind he prepared to leave the land he loved. The money for his passage to Jamaica might be raised by the early publication of some of his poems, in which he was encouraged by Gavin Hamilton. One of his friends in Irvine obtained for him a post as assistant overseer on the estate of Dr Douglas in Jamaica and all was ready for his departure.

His masonic friends lent weight to his own effort to get his poems printed and piece by piece he was able to let the printers in Kilmarnock have the results of his work. Of this period his memoirs record: "I threw off six hundred copies, for which I got subscriptions for about three hundred and fifty – My vanity was highly gratified by the reception I met with from the public: and besides, I pocketed, all expenses deducted, nearly £20". With this sum he was able to book a passage from Scotland to Jamaica.

It was at this time he visited the lodge at Tarbolton where much of his happiness lay, and here he sang a tearful farewell to the Master and the brethren:

The Farewell to the Brethren of Lodge St James, Tarbolton

Adieu! a heart-warm, fond adieu!
    Dear Brothers of the mystic tie!
Ye favoured ye enlightened few,
    Companions of my social joy!
Though I to foreign lands must hie,
    Pursuing Fortune's slidd'ry ba';
With melting heart and brimful eye,
    I'll mind you still, though far awa'.

Oft have I met your social band,
    And spent the cheerful festive night;
Oft, honoured with supreme command,
    Presided o'er the Sons of Light;
And by that hieroglyphic bright,
    Which none but craftsmen ever saw!
Strong mem'ry on my heart shall write
These happy scenes, when far awa'.

May freedom, harmony and love,
    Unite you in the grand design,
Beneath th' Omniscient Eye above,
    The glorious Architect divine!
That you may keep th' unerring line,
    Still rising by the plummet's law,
Till order bright completely shine,
    Shall be my prayer when far awa'.

And you farewell! whose merits claim,
    Justly, that highest badge to wear!
Heaven bless your honoured, noble name,
    To Masonry and Scotia dear!
A last request permit me here,
    When yearly ye assemble a',
One round, I ask it with a tear,
    To him, the Bard that's far awa'.

(slidd'ry = slippery)

In the last verse reference is made to Sir John Whitford, the Grand Master[3].

On 26 October 1786 Burns was admitted to the Lodge St John Kilwinning at Kilmarnock, as its Minutes record: "Robert Burns, poet from Mauchline, a member of Lodge St James Tarbolton was made an honorary member of this Lodge. (Signed Will. Parker)." As some of the brethren of this lodge had given great help to the poet in publishing the first edition of his poems it as only natural that the occasion should be marked by a song which was sung by Burns in the lodge; he possessed a fine bass voice. The reference to "Willie" meant Will Parker, the Master of the Lodge.

The Sons of Old Killie

Ye sons of old Killie, assembled by Willie,
    To follow the noble vocation,
Your thrifty old mother has scarce such another
    To sit in that honoured station.
I've little to say, but only to pray,
    As praying's the ton of your fashion:
A prayer from the Muse you may well excuse, –
    'Tis seldom her favourite passion.

Ye Powers who presided o'er the wind and the tide,
Who markèd each element's border;
Who formèd this frame with beneficent aim,
Whose sovereign statute is order!
Within this dear mansion may wayward contention
Or witherèd envy ne'er enter;
May secrecy round be the mystical bound,
And brotherly love be the centre!

(ton = mode, vogue)

The last four lines of this song must have remained in the poet's memory. A year later, on 23 August 1787, he wrote to the Lodge St James apologising for his absence in Edinburgh:

Men and Brethren,
I am truly sorry it is not in my power to be at your quarterly meeting. If I must be absent in body, believe me I shall be present in spirit. I support those who owe us monies, by bill or otherwise, will appear; I mean those we summoned. If you please I wish you would delay prosecuting defaulters till I come home. The Court is up, and I will be home before its sits down. In the meantime, to take a note of who appear and who do not, of our faulty debtors, will be right in my humble opinion; and those who confess debts and crave days, I think we shall spare them. Farewell.
Within this dear mansion may wayward Contention
Or witherèd envy ne'er enter;
May secrecy round be the mystical bound,
And brotherly love to be the centre!

Robt. Burns.

It was whilst Burns was waiting at Kilmarnock that there was another affair of the heart. It must be remembered that he had been rejected by Mr Armour and his daughter Jean and so he thought that he had reached the lowest point of despair. Possibly on a visit to see Gavin Hamilton he met Mary Campbell who was working as a servant to the Hamilton family at Mauchline. He fell in love with her and plighted his troth. In a solemn ceremony on the banks of a stream they exchanged Bibles. These were inscribed with verses therefrom and Burns signed them using not only his signature but also his Mason's mark. "Highland Mary", as Mary Campbell was called, then parted from Burns and went to Greenock on her way to the West Highlands, but fate intervened and she was destined never to get beyond Greenock. She became ill with a fever and died. The news of her death deeply affected the poet whose grief is expressed in the verse and songs which are amongst the most beautiful that he wrote. Truly it can be said that Mary's death broke his heart.

Burns in Edinburgh again!

It was on 31 July 1786 that the Kilmarnock edition of Burns' poems, already mentioned, had been published and his profit of about twenty pounds had enabled him to book his passage to Jamaica. His chest was packed and ready for despatch to Greenock when fate again intervened, this time in the form of a letter from Dr

Blacklock. It added weight to the persuasions of other masonic friends that the poet should publish a further edition of his works, this time in Edinburgh. He yielded to the kindly pressure and, on 28 November 1786, arrived in that city.

There he busied himself with the second edition, which was to include new poems. The publisher was to be William Creech, a leading member of Lodge Canongate Kilwinning; the printer was Brother William Smellie, who was a well-known author. Alexander Nasmyth, an artist who was also of the Canongate Lodge, was asked to paint Burns' portrait and, after several sittings, this was completed without charge. From it a third Canongate member, John Buego, made an engraving for inclusion in the book. Yet another Brother from the lodge reviewed the new edition, Henry McKenzie, then the editor of *The Lounger*, a literary periodical.

It can thus be seen that freemasons in Edinburgh greatly assisted the effort which had been urged upon him by his old masonic friends. With the praise of the leading members of Edinburgh society the new edition was assured of success. It was dedicated to "The Noblemen and Gentlemen of the Caledonian Hunt" then led by Lord Glencairn to whom he had been introduced by a friend and patron from the lodge in Ayrshire, James Dalrymple.

On 14 January 1787, Burns wrote to a masonic friend in Ayr, John Ballantyne:

> I went to a mason-lodge yesternight, where the Most Worshipful Grand Master Charters and all the Grand Lodge of Scotland visited. The meeting was numerous and elegant; all the different lodges in town were present in all their pomp. The Grand Master, who presided with great solemnity and honour to himself as a gentleman and mason, among other general toasts gave "Caledonia and Caledonia's Bard, Brother Burns", which rung through the whole assembly with multiplied honours and repeated acclamations. As I had no idea such a thing would happen I was downright thunderstruck, and trembling in every nerve made the best return in my power. Just as I had finished some of the Grand Officers said, so loud that I could hear, "Very well, indeed", which set me something to rights again.

The lodge which he had visited was Edinburgh St Andrew No. 48. He also went to a meeting of Lodge Canongate Kilwinning, as was thus recorded in its Minutes:

> The Right Worshipful Master having observed that Brother Burns was present in the Lodge, who is well known as a great poetic writer, and for a late publication of his works, which have been universally commended, submitted that he should be assumed a member of this Lodge, which was unanimously agreed to, and he was assumed accordingly.

As we would understand it, Burns was henceforth an honorary member of the lodge.

Many writers about Burns have repeated a tale that in Canongate Kilwinning he was made its "Poet Laureate". In 1846, fifty years after the poet's death, was published *A Winter with Robert Burns*. This book made positive mention of a picture, much reproduced, by Stewart Watson, of the poet being received in the lodge as Poet Laureate. (The original is to be seen in the Museum at Freemasons' Hall, Edinburgh.) The painting, which was the gift of Sir James Burnes, was discussed, at the request of the Grand Committee (of the Grand Lodge of Scotland) by selected brethren. Their report was unequivocal: the story promoted in *A Winter with Robert Burns* was fictitious. Since the office of Poet Laureate in Canongate

Kilwinning had not been created in Burns' lifetime, he could not have filled it. A critical study of Watson's pleasant picture, completed many years after Burns death, revealed that quite a few of the persons represented had never been members of the Craft, and that others could not possibly have been acquainted with the poet, either within or without Freemasonry.

In the year 1786-7, Burns was invited to a meeting at Professor Fergusson's at which he met several persons in the literary field. Here he spoke to a boy of fifteen who afterwards described the meeting and the appearance of the poet:

> His person was strong and robust; his manners rustic, not clownish; a sort of dignified plainness and simplicity, which received part of its effect, perhaps, from one's knowledge of his extraordinary talents.

The boy who wrote those words later became another of Scotland's distinguished sons, a poet, author and freemason – Sir Walter Scott.

It was on 21 April 1787 that the Edinburgh edition of the poems was published and just two days later Burns sold the copyright to William Creech. He then left the city to tour the border country with his friend Robert Ainslie. In his diary of this period he wrote: "19 May 1787. Spent the day at Mr. Grieve's – made a Royal Arch Mason at St Abbs Lodge (Eyemouth)". The Minutes record that Robert Ainslie and Robert Burns were made Royal Arch Masons and that the former paid one guinea admission dues but on account of Burns' remarkable poetic genius he was admitted gratis. The members considered themselves honoured by having a man of such shining ability for one of their companions.

After this tour Burns went home for a short while before returning to Edinburgh on 8 August 1787. He did not tarry long for on 25 August he left to tour the Highlands with his schoolmaster friend William Nichol. There followed a tour of Stirlingshire and then, after an enforced stay in Edinburgh with a dislocated knee, he returned to Mossgiel. Shortly afterwards he went through a form of marriage with Jean Armour and arranged to lease the farm at Ellisland by the side of the River Nith.

At Ellisland

This farm was owned by Mr Millar and it was only after a shrewd inspection that Burns decided to take the lease, which was on the most generous of terms. Still in existence and part of the wonderful countryside to the north of Dumfries, one can wander along the paths trodden by the poet when composing the famous tale of Tam o' Shanter. The farm was not immediately ready for occupation and in the intervening period he undertook training as an Excise Officer with a Mr James Finlay. James Finlay was a member of the Lodge St James at Tarbolton, and took over from Burns as Depute Master. At Mossgiel Mrs Burns also took some training in those duties which befell a farmer's wife and in farm management. The move to Ellisland was at last completed in the latter part of 1788, although Burns himself moved in and took up residence on 13 June. The house was in need of rebuilding and until this was done he could not ask Jean to join him. He worked hard and sometimes in loneliness he became depressed. This he expressed in verse in a letter to a masonic friend, Hugh Parker at Kilmarnock:

Wi' a' this care and a' this grief,
And sma', sma' prospects of relief,
And nought but peat-reek i' my head,
How can I write what ye can read? –
Tarbolton, twenty-fourth o'June,
Ye'll find me in a better tune;
But till we meet and weet our whistle,
Tak' this excuse for nae epistle.

(peat-reek = peat-smoke; weet = wet)

The date mentioned was, of course, St John the Baptist's day, on which James Finlay was to be installed as Burns' successor in the lodge. What with running his farm and his duties as an Excise Officer – these requiring him to travel a good deal on horseback – Burns would have been glad to give up his masonic appointment. But the Minutes of Lodge St James tell us that at meetings in October and November, he did in fact occupy the chair.

He was now living close to Dumfries, where several lodges were active. The oldest of these, then known as "Ye olde Lodge of Dumfries", claims precedence from 1575 and is now on the roll of the Grand Lodge of Scotland as Dumfries Lodge Kilwinning No. 53. Burns' friend, Dr Blacklock, was initiated in this Lodge and so at a later date was the poet's son, Robert, in 1833. Burns, however, joined the Dumfries Lodge St Andrews No. 179 (ceased working in 1805) on 27 December 1788. This was the feast day of St John the Evangelist and this might account for the verbal inaccuracies of the Minute recording the event:

St John's Day 27 December 1788. The Brethren having Selebrated the anniversary of St John in the usual manner and Brother Robt. Burns in Aelliesland of St Davids Strabolton Lodge No. 178 being present the Lodge unanimously assumed him a member of the Lodge being a Master mason he subscribed the regulation as a Member. Thereafter the Lodge was shut.

Tim Mackenzie.

The Last Years

Robert Burns remained a member of this lodge for the remainder of his short life. On 10 September 1791 the formal termination of the lease of Ellisland was signed and the family moved into a house in Dumfries on 11 November 1791. The house was in Wee Vennel, and he stayed there until May 1793 when he removed to the house in which he died. This is now a Burns memorial and is in Mill Vennel or Burns Street. He could now concentrate on his work as a gauger in the Excise Service, in which profession he gained promotion in February 1792 to the Dumfries Port Division. Two months later he had the honour of being made a member of the Royal Company of Archers of Edinburgh. In September of the same year began the correspondence with George Thompson which directly inspired Burns' interest in song-writing.

He had for some time contributed songs, and his thoughts on folk music, to an Edinburgh publication, Johnson's *Museum of Scottish Song*. Its first volume contained only one of Burns' songs, the now famous "Green grow the rashes O", but in March 1788 the second volume contained five. Thompson wrote to Burns and thereafter the poet contributed song and tunes directly to him. George Thompson was in touch with some of the great Austrian musicians, notably Pleyel and Kozeluch, and later Haydn. He paid them to write some of the music for the song. These composers were, in fact, freemasons and they all visited England to take part in the concerts organised by Salomon, who was a member of the Pilgrim Lodge which still meets in London.

Burns sent many songs to Thompson, and without any shadow of doubt these have added considerably to the musical heritage of Scotland. The work provided him with great pleasure but little money. In 1793 he sent to Thompson the words of "Scots wha hae", one of the greatest national songs ever published. In these years he maintained attendance at his Dumfries lodge which, however, did not meet as often as that at Tarbolton. Between 1791 and the date of his death on 21 July 1796 it met on sixteen occasions. The Minutes record that Robert was present at eleven of those meetings.

1791	27 December
1792	6 February, 14 and 31 May, 5 June, 22 and 30 November
1793	30 November
1794	29 November
1796	29 January, 14 April.

His absence in 1795 may be explained by the fact that he was working as supervisor in the Excise Department and was also active in organising the Dumfries Volunteers. In August 1791 the foundation stone was laid for the new bridge across the River Nith. The lodges in Dumfries were closely associated with this work and the ceremony was conducted by Alexander Fergusson of Craigdarroch, Esq., "Grand Master of the masonic lodges constituted in the Southern District of Scotland".

The meetings which he did attend included a few of special interest:
5 June 1792: "Ed. Andrews of the Dragoons and John Syme Esq. of Barncailizie were admitted Brethren without fees." Burns was a visitor to John Syme's house and here, using his diamond, he engraved a goblet with the verse:

> There's death in the cup – sae beware!
> Nay, more – there is danger in touching,
> But wha can avoid the fell snare?
> The man and his wine's sae bewitching!

28 January 1796: "Mr James Georgeson merchant in Liverpool, appeared and who being recommended by Bro. Burns was admitted apprentice."
14 April 1796: Robert Burns attended lodge for the last time to see his friend Captain Adam Gordon initiated into the Craft. He had given his promise that he would attend and he kept loyally to that promise.

He was now seriously ill, and on the advice of Dr Maxwell he went to a small spa on the Solway Firth to sea-bathe and to take the waters. It was here that he spent the last two weeks of his life. On the morning of his departure for Brow Well he wrote to James Johnson: "This protracting, slow, consuming illness will, I doubt much, my dear friend, arrest my sun before he has well reached his middle career". He returned to his home on 18 July and on the 21st he passed to the Grand Lodge Above.

The cause of his death has best been summarised by Sir James Crichton Browne in an excellent short book dedicated to Sir Robert Bruce, President of the Burns Federation, and entitled *Burns from a New Point of View:* "It will not, I think, he disputed that Burns died of rheumatic endocarditis, with the origin of which alcohol had nothing to do."

Retrospect

Throughout his short life of thirty-seven years Burns created a collection of poems and songs which have been translated into many languages. He is quoted as much in Russia and America as in his beloved and native Scotland. The appeal lies in his complete understanding of humanity and an enduring and simple faith, learned at his father's knee. While his fame is not due to the fact that he was a freemason, it is noteworthy that his numerous friends in Ayrshire, Edinburgh, and Dumfries were mostly brethren of the lodges in which he worked or which he visited. Many of these he remembered in verse and to others he dedicated his works.

There are many references to Freemasonry in his poems, other than those already quoted. From "Address to the De'il" comes:

> When Masons' mystic word an' grip,
> In storms an' tempests raise you up,
> Some cock or cat your rage maun stop,
>   Or, strange to tell!
> The youngest Brother ye wad whip
>   Aff straught to hell!
>
>   [maun = must]

John Wilson was the schoolmaster of Tarbolton and Secretary of Lodge St James. He also ran a small grocery store and fancied himself as a student of medicine. In the early part of 1785 he crossed swords in a literary sense with Burns, who thought that the parade of his medical knowledge was rather overbearing and pompous. After the lodge closed he walked home and wrote the poem "Death and Doctor Hornbook". In it Burns held Wilson to such ridicule that he left Tarbolton for Glasgow.[4]

Of the song "The Happy Trio" Burns wrote: "The air is Masterton's, the song is mine, and William Nichol found the Maut [malt]". The song recalls happy occasions spent in the company of his masonic friends.

Tam Samson was a well-known Kilmarnock sportsman and a member of the local lodge. He is commemorated in the poem "Tam Samson's Elegy" which Burns wrote on hearing the rumour that Samson had died. This rumour proved false, whereupon the poet wrote an additional verse:

> Go, Fame, and canter like a filly,
> Through a' the streets and neuks o' Killie,
> Tell every social, honest billie

To cease his grievin',
For yet, unskaithed by Death's gleg gullie,
Tam Samson's Leevin'!

(Killie = Kilmarnock; neuks = nooks; billie = fellow;
unskaithed = unhurt; gleg = sharp; gullie = knife; leevin' = living)

In passing it might be mentioned that Tam Samson outlived Burns!

A four-line stanza was added to another poem especially to meet the need in a masonic lodge. Entitled "The Big-Bellied Bottle":

Then fill up a bumper, and make it o'erflow,
And honours masonic prepare for to throw;
May every true Brother of the Compass and Square
Have a big-bellie'd bottle when harass'd with care!

Many of his masonic friends had passed away before Burns himself received his "Highland Welcome". Those he held dear to him he remembered in verse. Robert Aiken who worked diligently to secure subscriptions for the Kilmarnock edition of Burns's poetry, and to whom "The Cotter's Saturday Night" is dedicated, is thus remembered:

Epitaph for Robert Aiken, Esq.

Know thou, O stranger to the fame
Of this much-loved, much-honoured name,
(For none that knew him need be told)
A warmer heart Death ne'er made cold.

To John Dove, the innkeeper at Mauchline, where the lodge sometimes met:

Here lies Johnny Pidgeon:
What was his religion?
Whae'er desired to ken,
To some other warl'
Maun follow the carl,
For here Johnny Pidgeon had nane!

(warl' = world; carl = old man)

The Earl of Glencairn gave considerable assistance to Burns, whom he respected and honoured. His early death is remembered in an elegy:

The mother may forget the child
That smiles sae sweetly on her knee;
But I'll remember thee, Glencairn,
And a' that thou hast done for me!

Sir John Whiteford (the Grand Master referred to in the last verse of "The Farewell to the Brethren of Lodge St James, Tarbolton"), James Tennent, Alexander

Campbell, Gavin Hamilton and many others were either written to in verse or remembered in epitaph.

Memories and treasured possessions of Burns are in museums all over the world, and yet to the small town of Tarbolton many brethren of the mystic tie come each year. In the Bachelors' Club and in the masonic centre they are shown some of the lodge furniture which was in use in his time, and which is still used today.

Sadly the meetings of St Andrew's Lodge in Dumfries became more and more infrequent and eventually ceased altogether in 1804. The Grand Lodge finally deleted it from the roll in 1816. Its artefacts came up for auction in 1879 and were acquired by the then Grand Secretary. This was reported to the Grand Master Mason, Sir Michael Shaw Stewart, who immediately paid the purchase price, and presented them to the Grand Lodge where they now lie.

In the British Museum is an item which is of interest to all concerned with Robert Burns – his famous punch bowl. It was given to him by James Armour as a wedding present when he at last married his daughter, Jean. The union was officially recognised by the Mauchline Kirk Session on 5 August 1788. As Robert fought to make a home for her at Ellisland he wrote:

> Of a' the airts the wind can blaw,
> I dearly like the west,
> For there the bonnie lassie lives,
> The lassie I lo'e best:
> There wild woods grow, and rivers row
> And mony a hill between;
> But day and night my fancy's flight
> Is ever wi' my Jean.

(airts = directions)

The bowl of Inverary marble was a natural present for James Armour to give for he was by trade a stone-mason and could easily have made it. There is no doubt that Burns put it to good use. Dr Currie wrote of one occasion in *The Works of Burns* (1800), vol. 1: "he produced at the same time his punch bowl, made of Inverary marble, and, mixing the spirit with water and sugar filled their glasses, and invited them to drink".

After Robert's death in 1796 his widow directed that the bowl should be sent to Alexander Cunningham in Edinburgh. This was done by his brother Gilbert with a letter:

Dumfries, 16th January 1801

Dear Sir,

I herewith send you a small punch-bowl in Inverary marble. To present you with so paltry a vessel of such base material requires some explanation. Mrs Burns has for some time expressed wish to present you with some small testimony of the sense she has of your friendly attachment to her children as well as to their father. I have advised her that as this bowl has acquired some celebrity from Dr Currie's having connected it with his description of the social powers as well as habits of its former owner, it will be an agreeable present to you, and I hope it will reach you while Mr Syme is with you, that in his company the melancholy luxury of the recollection of joys that are past may be produced in your mind so susceptible of tender impressions.

I am, Dear Sir,
Yours most truly,
Gilbert Burns.

The Mausoleum in Dumfries Churchyard

Cunningham must have been pleased to have this present, for he immediately had silver mounts made for the rim and for the foot of the bowl. On that which surrounds the rim is engraved an appropriate quotation from a Burns poem:

> But ye whom social pleasure charms,
> Whose hearts the tide of kindness warms,
> Who hold your being on the terms
> "Each aid the others"
> Come to my Bowl, come to my arms'
> My FRIENDS, my BROTHERS!

Cunningham died on 27 January 1812 and there is no evidence of what happened to the bowl while it was in his possession. In the Edinburgh Press some four years later, however, an auction sale was advertised to take place on Saturday, 21 January 1816. Ballantyne, the auctioneer, records in his diary that the sale raised some five hundred pounds and that the bowl was sold for eighty-four pounds.

The bowl next appeared in London where it was apparently in use at a tavern in the Strand owned by a man named Cochran. It is fortunate that Cochran pawned the bowl and sold the ticket to Archibald Hastie who immediately redeemed the pledged item for the sum of forty pounds. This occurred in about the year 1830 and in April 1858 the Trustees of the British Museum were pleased to accept the Burns bowl into their safe keeping at the bequest of Mr Hastie. It has remained in their keeping ever since and is on display.

After the death of the poet on 21 July 1796 his body lay in state at the Town Hall until 26 July. The funeral took place on a fine day, the local Volunteers according full military honours. Some thousands of people were present at the interment in a quiet corner of St Michael's churchyard and on the grave was placed a plain tombstone bearing simply the name and age of the poet. A public subscription was launched in 1813, raising a large sum of money which enabled a mausoleum to be

93

built on an elevated site in the churchyard. The remains of Robert Burns were transferred to it with solemn dignity on 19 September 1815.

Conclusion

Burns, without doubt, gained considerable advantages from Freemasonry and he played his full part in the work and in propagating the message which brethren have to offer. He enjoyed his membership and it contributed to his experience in that it enabled him to meet with many persons of great intelligence and from different stations in life. His talents were encouraged, and among his friends his manners were refined and his thinking stimulated.

At his father's knee he learned to love his God and all created things. By the study of the Volume of the Sacred Law he was able to dedicate himself to a truthful and honest way of life, even in the most difficult circumstances. Further, in the ritual of the lodge, and possibly in the dancing classes held in Tarbolton, he acquired a deportment which enabled him to meet with persons of the highest social position when he made his visits to Edinburgh. Above all, his meeting with such a wide circle of friends and people enabled him to gain an understanding of philosophy and humanity.

To the brethren of the Lodge Tarbolton he owed much. He was invited by them to share their tables, they motivated the publication of the Kilmarnock edition of the poems and, when his star was just beginning its ascent, it was the advice given to him by masonic friends which urged him on his way to Edinburgh.

In a tribute to Burns the late Lord Rosebery said: "Burns' true life began with his death. With the poet passed all that was gross or impure; the clear spirit stood revealed and soared at once to its accepted placed among the fixed stars in the firmament of the rare immortals."

As Freemasons we can and do honour his name and join with him in the great thought expressed in the poem "Is there, For Honest Poverty", better known as "A Man's a Man for a' that".

> Then let us pray that come it may,
> As come it will for a' that,
> That sense and worth, o'er a' the earth,
> May bear the gree, and a' that.
> For a' that, and a' that,
> It's coming yet, for a' that,
> That man to man, the warld o'er,
> Shall brothers be for a' that.

(bear the gree = win the victory; warld = world)

(The spelling, punctuation and style of print varies in the different editions of Burns' poems. All quotations in this paper have been taken from The Poetical Works of Robert Burns, Frederick Warne & Co. London and New York, n.d. Printed in Edinburgh.)

ACKNOWLEDGEMENTS

To the Curators of the "clay biggin" and Burns centre at Alloway.
To the Curator for the Bachelors' Club at Tarbolton for his detailed explanation for dancing the reel with the lady from Mexico.

To the brethren at the Tarbolton Masonic Centre for all their assistance and for the Historical
   Review 1771-1976 prepared by Past Master John Weir.
To the Curator and his wife at the Ellisland Farm for their kindness in showing me the farm
   and the walk made by Robert Burns by the lovely River Nith.
To the brother fisherman who permitted me to cast a fly across the water where the poet him-
   self had fished.
To the keeper of the Burns House in Mill Vennel or Burns Street, Dumfries, for his kindly
   explanations and help.
To the librarians of the Mitchel Library in Glasgow where they have a marvellous collection
   of documents and books concerning their national bard.
To the Grand Secretary and staff of the Grand Lodge of Scotland for their kindness when I
   went to see the Burns relics at Freemason's Hall.

REFERENCES

The *Poetical Works of Robert Burns* (Frederick Warne & Co., London and New York, n.d.)
Burns from a New Point of View, by Sir James Crichton Browne
A Winter with Robert Burns (1846)
The Lodge of St James Tarbolton Kilwinning No. 135, by John Weir
Brithers A', by Peter Esslemont (1945)
Robert Burns' Commonplate Book, 1783–1785
"The Punchbowl of Robert Burns", *British Museum Quarterly,* vol. 23 (1961)
The Works of Burns, by Dr James Currie (1800)
Poems in the Scottish Dialect, by Robert Burns (The Kilmarnock Edition, 1786)
Burnsiana, the quarterly journal of the Burns Federation (in the Mitchell Library of
   Scotland)

EDITOR'S FOOTNOTES TO CHAPTER TWELVE

1. The Burns family were eleven (11) years at Mount Oliphant.
2. There is no evidence to support this view.
3. No. The Master of the Lodge at that time was Brother Montgomerie of Coilsfield.
4. John Wilson (Hornbook) remained in the village for several years before moving to
   Glasgow.

Chapter Thirteen

Lecture Two

THE MASONIC GENIUS OF ROBERT BURNS

Benjamin Ward Richardson
This paper was first published in the Transactions
of the Quatuor Coronati Lodge, 1892.

When I speak of the Masonic genius of Robert Burns, I mean that his genius, which is universally admitted, partakes of the genius of Masonic order or type. In this discourse I shall consider him first from this point of view. Next, I shall speak of his poetic genius as appealing primarily to the Masonic brotherhood, and as fostered and fed by that fraternity. I shall then proceed to treat of his love for the brotherhood as manifested in the productions of his poetic genius. Finally, I shall for a few moments dwell on the tendency and tenure of his work as Masonic in quality in the higher and nobler, shall I not say the highest and noblest, forms of Masonic liberty and moral amplitude. This will divide my subject into four sections or parts, and will enable brethren who may join in the discussion to fix on particular points as they follow what I shall venture to lay before them.

In studying the first section of this division – the genius of Masonry in relation to the natural genius of the man – we must know the man from the first, know him from his own heart. In an order or fraternity like Masonry there is a true, a deep, and subtle genius which holds it together; and that the order may be held together there must be, in a greater or lesser degree, the same kind of genius in every individual member. All fraternities of might and effect and endurance, whether they be considered good or bad by outsiders, must be constructed on this plan. Orders, in fact, are composed of men born to aptitudes befitting the order. There are, of course, exceptions to this general rule. There are in every fraternity members who are perfectly indifferent; there are members who are merely converts; and there are, in all great combinations, a few who may even be inimical. But on the whole the strongest societies have for their centre an overwhelming unity, at the head of which are they who are particularly bound to the principles that are at stake, and who come into the mastery of those principles by what is naturally a common bond. In this position Robert Burns stands as regards the Masonic bond and unity. Masonry, when he found it, was akin to his native genius; it was to him that touch of nature which makes all akin.

For the birth of this sympathy we have to turn to the best picture we can get of the poet while his nature was being moulded into the form it took as Mason and poet. Fortunately for us, owing to the interposition of a very remarkable man, who is now too much forgotten, we have an account of this period of the poet's life from the poet himself. The scholar who obtained this treasure was Dr John Moore, the father of that illustrious Sir John Moore, hero of Corunna, on whom Wolfe wrote the immortal poem beginning,

"Not a drum was heard nor a funeral note,
As his corse to the ramparts we hurried,
Not a soldier discharged a farewell shot
O'er the grave where our hero we buried."

Dr Moore, whose life I have recently written, and of whom I present three portraits for your inspection, was by profession a physician, residing first in Glasgow and finally in London; but he added to his Esculapian gifts those of the traveller, the man of the world, and the industrious writer. He was in France with the Duke of Hamilton before the days of the great Revolution, and with the same clearness of foresight as his friend Smollett, predicted the great event that must follow from what he beheld in progress. Again, he was in Paris in the early days of the great Revolution itself; heard the first shots fired at the Tuilleries; attended the meetings of the National Assembly; and left the finest description of Marat, whom he knew personally, that has ever been written on that famous infamous person. His journal of the days of the Revolution has been more cribbed from, without acknowledgement, than most works of original men. But he was more than the journalist of striking events; he was himself an artist in letters, and his story "Zelucco" was the inspiration of the poem "Childe Harold", which Byron left to the admiring world. Still further, Dr Moore was of biographic taste, and was anxious, on all suitable occasions, to get from their prime sources the histories of remarkable men. Thus it was he got from Robert Burns himself that account of his, Burns', early days with which, I doubt not, most of you are familiar. Gilbert Burns, brother of the poet, says that in this narrative the poet set off some of his early companions "in too consequential a manner", which is perhaps too true, for poets are apt to be poets all over, in prose as in verse; anyway, there is rendered in this composition the fact which chiefly concerns us, that companionship of the brotherly type was the early love of the after Mason. Burns rejoiced in all social gatherings, and cared nothing whatever for his daily work when he was encircled, in the evening of the day, with his friends whom, in love or in war, in song or in story, he impetuously led. He was mystic from the first, and breathed poetry before he knew it himself. Like Pope:

"He lisped in numbers, or the numbers came."

He was living at Tarbolton with his family when these faculties, belonging to his seventeenth year, developed themselves. He possessed, he says, a curiosity, zeal, and intrepid dexterity that recommended him as a proper second, and he felt as much pleasure in being in the secret of half the loves of Tarbolton as ever did statesman in knowing the intrigues of half the courts of Europe. He felt that to the sons and daughters of poverty, "the ardent hope, the stolen interview, the tender farewell, are the greatest and most delicious parts of their enjoyments". This was a glance at the loves of the simple: he found it to apply, later on, to other mysteries, and in all cases his heart beat sympathetically to the sentiment.

In his nineteenth year he made a change in his life which is curious, symbolically, and perhaps in relation to after Masonic work of the speculative rather than the working character. He spent his nineteenth summer on a smuggling coast, a good distance from home, at a noted school, to learn mensuration, surveying, and dialling. Here, although he took part in scenes which had better have been avoided, he went on "with a high hand" at his geometry, "till the sun entered Virgo, which was always a carnival in his bosom", and then in a few weeks he left his school to return home. But he had considerably improved, and from his studies had certainly learned the use of the tools of a Mason, the rule, the compass, the level, and the skerritt.

All this was congenial towards Masonry in its form of speculative mystery, and we need not, therefore, be surprised that it was not long before he joined our ancient order. There was, at the time of his residence at Tarbolton, a Masonic Lodge called St David.[1] The harmony which ought to exist in all Lodges of the Craft does not seem to have been perfect in this one. There had been another Lodge in Tarbolton, known as St James, and some discordant elements might have come down from that Lodge to St Davids, which, for a time, superseded it. Be that as it may, St David's had the honour of receiving the young Scottish poet into its bosom. Burns was initiated in Lodge St David, Tarbolton, on 4 July 1781, he being then in his twenty-third year. He became from that moment one of the most devoted of Masons. In every way Masonry was congenial to his mind. There was in it a spirit of poetry which was all the sweeter to him because it was concealed, and there was in it the fact of something done which the best in the world copied from without knowing the source of the inspiration; something like that which Shelley afterwards, unconsciously as applied to this subject, expressed in the exquisite song to the skylark:

"Like a poet hidden
    In the light of thought,
Singing hymns unbidden
    Till the world is wrought
To sympathy with hopes
    And fears it heeded not."

and which Burns himself, in another form and measure, expressed in the lines:

"The social, friendly, honest man,
    Whate'er he be,
'Tis he fulfils great Nature's plan,
    And none but he."

Burns had no sooner been initiated into Masonry than he threw himself into work connected with it with his whole heart. He found, nevertheless, that even among Masons there may be discord. The old feud in the Lodge St David increased, and came, at last, to such a pitch, that a sharp division took place. In the year 1782 a number of the members of the Lodge seceded, and re-formed the old and almost forgotten Lodge St James of Tarbolton. Burns was amongst the seceders, and the newly-formed Lodge was destined, largely by his warm adhesion to it, to become one of the most famous historical Lodges Scottish Masonry ever boasted of. In this Lodge the poet found poetry, and in it, above all other prizes in the world, he found friendship. This fact leads me, naturally, to the second division of my paper: the fostering care he experienced as a poet from Masonic communion and enthusiasm.

By the time Burns joined the Lodge at Tarbolton he was a poet. He was not a poet of any wide renown, but he had written poems which some of his immediate circle of friends admired. His life up to this period had been one of great strain and poverty. Born in a little cottage near Alloway Kirk, on the Doon, in Ayrshire, he had moved with his parents, when about seven years of age, to a farm in the parish of Ayr, called Mount-Oliphant. The farm was a ruinous affair. Here he worked on the land as a farm-boy for twelve years, after which the family passed, with no better fortune, to another farm, called Lochlea, in the parish of Tarbolton. Robert worked like the rest on this farm, but he was not exclusively engaged on farm labour. He went, as already told, to a sea coast place, Kirk Oswald[2], where he learned mensuration and other parts of arithmetic, which ultimately fitted him for the duties of an excise officer, and on the whole he picked up, at Kirk Oswald parish school, much information that served him well, with some tricks which did not serve him so well. He returned to the farm at Lochlea in his twentieth year; resumed work with his brother Gilbert, fell in love with a servant-maid, who jilted him, and led rather a wild life altogether. He and his brother tried their hands at flax-farming at the neighbouring village of Irvine[3], but during a New Year's day carousal the flax shop took fire and the whole stock was burnt up. Worse still, he got into bad company and into some disrepute.

Affairs at Lochlea went wrong with the excellent father of the poet, and in February, 1784, that good man died. The loss of his father incited the poet to a better life, and he and his brother took a larger farm at a place called Mossgiel[4], in the parish of Mauchline, near Tarbolton. The farming project failed, and good resolutions failed with it.

Our Brother the poet Burness, for he assumed the shorter name of Burns later on, was not at the moment of his career at which we have arrived, in a very happy or a very hopeful condition. He was poverty stricken, he was reckless, he had sent into the world an illegitimate child, and he was looked upon askance by those friends about him, who considered good morals the first of acquirements. Yet, with it all, he was not the absolute rake or prodigal which many have depicted him. He had availed himself of what advantages had come before him. He had been for a short time blessed by the instruction of a tutor named Murdoch, from whom he had learned among other things French, in which language he greatly delighted, and he had gathered together various classical and romantic books which he read with the avidity a nature such as his alone experiences. He had seen a little of the world at Kirk Oswald, and he had acquired some knowledge of the exact sciences. But above all, he was a poet and a Mason.

Opinions have differed since his death, as they differed in his own time and amongst his own friends, on the point whether he did ill or well joining the Lodge in Tarbolton. Masonry was rather popular in Scotland, but many thought that Robert Burness had joined it, not because of the goodness there was in it, but because of

"The wale o' cocks for fun and drinkin',"

and in this view there was much sense for sober going people, since it cannot be denied that Scotia's drink was freely floated in the Lodges, when refreshments followed the serious business of labour. Moreover, Robert himself, at his twenty-third year, was a sufficient cause for alarm among his friends. He was, physically, not well. He had frequent dull headaches, and he was laying the seeds for those conditions of faintness and palpitations of the heart, which as his brother Gilbert tells us, were the bodily burthens of after years.

He was, moreover, at this time, exceedingly unbridled in his tastes. He was the prime spirit of a bachelors' club, which, although the expenses were limited to threepence per bachelor each night, was an assembly that did not particularly raise him in public estimation[5]; and he was always in love, not with one object of affection, but with any and many, according to fancy, investing, by his fancy, as Brother Gilbert inform us, each of his loves with such a stock of charms, all drawn from the plentiful stores of his imagination, that there was often a great dissimilitude between the fair captivator as she appeared to others and as she seemed when bedecked with the attributes he gave to her. Up to this time he was not given to intoxication, and when, with his brother and family he entered into partnership for the farm of Mossgiel, he contributed his share of expenses, and lived most frugally. He had written songs and other poetical pieces, which pleased those who surrounded him, and the poems had accumulated to a goodly number, but they were buried in necessity, and it is very doubtful if by his own efforts they would ever have been brought to light.

Day by day his adversity grew more and more pressing. At last a crisis. Amongst his many loves there was one who held to him to the end the most firmly, namely, Jean Armour, and with her love went so far it could no longer be concealed. In the strait the lovers came to a determination. They entered into a legal acknowledgement of "an irregular private marriage", and it was proposed that Burns should at once proceed to Jamaica as an assistant overseer on the estate of Dr Douglas[6]. Strangely, the parents of Jean Armour objected to the acceptance of the marriage, under the impression that great as had been the folly of Jean she might live to do better than tie herself for life to a scapegrace. To Burns this slight was intolerable, although in a kind of contrition he seemed to bend to it. It settled his resolve, he would go to Jamaica, and by honest work would make up for past misfortune.

It happened that much time was required before he could make a start for his new sphere of labour, and, meanwhile, as preparations were going on something else occurred, on which, as on a pivot, the fate and fame of Robert Burns turned. In the Lodge of St James, Tarbolton, there was an important member, a writer to the signet, living near by at Mauchline, and the landlord of the farm of Mossgiel. This was Gavin Hamilton, a happy-go-lucky, warm-hearted, merry fellow, much attached to the ploughman poet, some of whose effusions he had heard in song at least, and towards whom he entertained a sincere admiration. Hamilton suggested that Burns should collect and publish an edition of his poems, and that the expense should be met by a subscription. The plan was after the poet's own desire, I may say fervent desire. He longed to leave his name to posterity, and, in fact, cared for little else. The ordinary life was to him already a burden, but the idea of immortal fame was something worth living for, and was even worth the weariness of the world. He seized, therefore, on the proposal with avidity. It was early in the year of 1786, and his vessel for Jamaica would not sail until November; let then the proposal, of all things, be carried out.

With all his faults Burns stood high in his Lodge of St James, at Tarbolton. In 1784 he was made Depute Master, Major General Montgomery being Worshipful

Master. In 1785 he attended Lodge nine times, and acted many times, if not every time, as Master. In 1786 he attended nine times, and at the second meeting[7], held on 1 March, passed and raised his brother Gilbert. How well he fulfilled the duties of his office is told by no less a person than the famous metaphysical scholar, Dugald Stewart, who had a neighbouring country residence at Catrine. Stewart specially commends the ready wit, happy conception and fluent speech of the Depute Master of Lodge St James. There can be no doubt that the Lodge, in return, became responsible altogether for the issue of the first volume of poems of Robert Burns, not as an official act, but as an act of personal friendship for their talented brother; and, under their initiative, he went to Kilmarnock, in order to see through the Press the new and now precious first edition of poems dated 16 April 1786. Whilst residing in Kilmarnock[8], he met with the warmest reception and encouragement from the Masonic brethren there. He became a visitor of their Lodge St John at once, and on 26 October 1786, was admitted an honorary member. The brethren of this Lodge assisted him also substantially in his venture. Brother Major Parker subscribed to 35 copies of the book, and Robert Muir, another of the brethren of St John's, to 75 copies, whilst a third brother, John Wilson, printed and published the volume. In short, the first edition was in every sense such a Masonic edition, we may almost declare that but for Masonry the poems of Robert Burns, now disseminated over all the world, had merely been delivered to the winds as the mental meanderings of a vulgar and disreputable Scottish boor[9]. Thus, the genius of Masonry discovered and led forth the genius of one of the greatest of the poets of Scotland.

The good genius of masonry did not end at this point. It brought out the volume of poems, and made the author master of a little balance of money for his work; but, alas, the return was not sufficient to prevent the evil fate that would separate him from all he loved best[10]. He was still pursued by ill fortune. His little bit of luggage was on its way to Greenock, he following it, playing at hide-and-seek, and wishing Jamaica at the bottom of the sea, when a letter reached him again from a brother mason[11], a gentle blind brother, with a taste for the muses, Brother Dr Blacklock, suggesting that a new edition of the Kilmarnock poems should be published in Edinburgh, and that their author should go to that fair city and superintend the undertaking. Burns at once responded, and on 26 November, instead of being on the sea for the West Indies, he was in the modern Athens, and in the midst of enthusiastic friends, all warmed to friendship by the mystical fire. Here things went grandly. Henry Mackenzie, a good mason and good writer, author of "The Man of Feeling", announced through a paper, called the *Lounger,* that a new poet had been born to Scotland; and David Ramsay, editor of the *Evening Courant,* another brother, represented him to his world of letters as:

"The Prince of Poets, an o' pleughmen."

And so this Prince of Poets ploughed his way into the best circles of Auld Reekie. He was at once great in the Masonic Lodges. The Worshipful Grand Master Charteris, at the Lodge of St Andrew, proposed as a toast, "Caledonia and Caledonia's Bard Brother Burns", "a toast", the Bard writes, "which rang through the whole assembly, with multiplied honours and repeated acclamations"; while he, having no idea such a thing would happen, "was downright thunderstruck, and trembling in every nerve" made the best return in his power. Jamaica vanished!

Early next year, 1 February 1787, the Edinburgh edition of the poems being well in hand, Burns was admitted by unanimous consent a brother of the Canongate Kilwinning Lodge, in which on the first of the following month the Master – Fergusson of Craigdarrock – dignified him as Poet Laureate of the brotherhood[12], and assigned him a special poet's throne. The time now quickly arrived, 21 April, for the appearance of the new volume. The members of the Caledonian Hunt, under the leadership of Lord Glencairn, to whom the poet was introduced by Brother Dalrymple, subscribed liberally, and altogether a subscription list of 2,000 copies was secured, the Masonic influence again leading the way. "Surely", says an anonymous writer on this subject, "a son of the Rock", as he styled himself, but whom I have since found to have been Mr James Gibson, of Liverpool, and not himself a Mason, "surely never book came out of a more Masonic laboratory. Publisher, printer, portrait painter, and engraver of the portrait were a rare class of men – all characters in their way – and all Masons." Creech was the publisher, Smellie was the printer, Alexander Nasmyth was the painter, and Beugo was the engraver, each and all masons of the staunchest quality. Under such support the poems were bound to go, and they went, carrying their author with them into the glory he most desired.

As it is not my business to dwell on the life of Burns out of its Masonic encircling, I need not dwell on his later career; his flirtations with Clarinda, his love with Mary Campbell; his journeyings and jollifications; his melancholy and his remorse; his marriage with Jean Armour; his failure as a farmer at Ellisland; his entrance into the excise; his residence at Dumfries; his final intemperance[13] and his early death on 21 July 1796. Let it be sufficient to add that Lodge St Abbs at Eyemouth made him a Royal Arch Mason, omitting his fees and considering themselves honoured by having a man of such shining abilities as one of their companions; that when he settled in Dumfries, the Lodge of St Andrew received him with open arms; and that to him ever, to use the words of Mr Gibson, "Masonry held out an irresistible hand of friendship".

I come now to the third point to which, Worshipful Master, I would direct the mind of the Lodge – the love of the poet for the brotherhood, as represented in his poetical works.

There are at least eight poems in which Masonry is directly connected with the theme of the poem or song. A short epistle in verse to Brother Dr Mackenzie, informing him that Lodge St James will meet on St John's day, is racy and refers to a controversy on morals which had been going on in the little circle. An elegy to Tam Samson relates to a famous seedsman, sportsman, and curler, but above all a Mason of the Kilmarnock Lodge, and a sterling friend of all who knew him in friendship's mysteries.

> "The brethren o' the mystic level
> May hing their heads in waefu' bevel,
> While by their nose the tears will revel
>   Like ony bead.
> Death's gien the Lodge an unco' devel,
>   Tam Samson's dead."

In like manner, but with a tender sweetness and more subdued verse, he writes another elegy on one to whom he was bound by the mystic tie, Sir James Hunter

Blair. The poem is finely conceived. The poet supposes himself wandering in some secluded haunt:

> "The lamp of day, with ill-presaging glare,
> Dim, cloudy, sinks beneath the western wave,
> Th' inconstant blast howls through the darkening air,
> And hollow, whistles in the rocky cave."

The moon then rises "in the livid east", and among the cliffs the stately form of Caledonia appears "dropped in pensive woe". "The lightning of her eyes" is imbued in tears; her spear is reversed; her banner at her feet. So attuned she sings her sorrow for the loss of her son and the grief of her sons, not omitting the sons of light and science:

> "A weeping country joins a widow's tear,
> The helpless poor mix with the orphan's cry;
> The drooping arts surround their patron's bier,
> And grateful science heaves the heartfelt sigh."

In an epistle to his publisher, William Creech, whose Masonic virtues I have already noted, we get just a glimpse into Lodge Kilwinning, Edinburgh, when Willie, that is Creech, is on his travels in London. "Willie's awa'."

> "Now worthy Gregory's latin face,
> Tytler's and Greenfield's modest grace,
> Mackenzie Stewart, sic a brace,
> They a' maun meet some ither place. Willie's awa'!"

Gregory of the Latin face was the famous Dr James Gregory, perhaps the purest Latin writer medicine ever produced in his country, but better known as the inventor of the most nauseous, and yet one of the most useful medicines – Gregory's powder. Greenfield was the eminent Professor of Rhetoric; and Stewart the illustrious Dugald.

"Willie brew'd a peck of maut" is a Masonic song of genius. Willie was Brother William Nicol, of the High School, Edinburgh, with whom the poet made a tour to the Highlands; Allan was Brother Alan Masterton, and Rob was Brother the Poet himself; three Masons holding an informal Lodge[14] at Nichol's place at Moffat during the summer vacation. It was such a joyous meeting that each in his own way celebrated it; Willie – Nichol – and the maut, Rob – Burns – with the song, and Allan – Masterton – with the music.

The poem of Death and Dr Hornbook is of Masonic origin. Hornbook was Brother Wilson, schoolmaster of Tarbolton, and a member of the Lodge, who took to reading medical books and dabbling in physic. One night, after going from labour to refreshment, Wilson paraded his medical knowledge and skill too loudly to miss the watchful Robert, and Robert, on his way home, was accompanied by this mixture of pedantry and physic to a certain point, where they shook hands and parted[15]. Left alone, the old fancies of goblins and spirits came on the poet; Death came, and after a conversation with that reaper, the following satire on the poor dominie was composed. These circumstances, Gilbert Burns says, his brother related as he repeated the verses to him the next afternoon, while Gilbert was holding the plough and Robert was letting the water off the field beside him. How the poem took when it was first published is a matter of history. It settled poor Brother Wilson for good as a self-constituted doctor at Tarbolton, the verse beginning with the words, "A bonnie lass ye kenn'd her name", telling with potent effect.

Wilson, I believe, was the only Mason Burns lampooned, and he without enmity. Wilson, however, had to leave Tarbolton[16], and, retreating to Glasgow, became clerk of the Gorbals parish, and lived until 1839, half-a-century after the Tarbolton exodus. Cromek, one of the writers on Burns*, who knew Wilson in his later days, says Wilson had so little pedantry about him that a man who never read the poem would scarcely discover any, and I have heard others who also knew him make the same observation.

*Cromek, a Yorkshireman, an art publisher, engraver, and in some sense, an artist, went to Scotland, ten years after the poet's death, to collect materias for a volume on Burns, as a kind of supplement to four volumes that had already been written by Dr Currie. The volume was entitled the "Reliques of Burns", and was published by Cadell and Davies in 1808.

The song entitled "The sons of old Killie", beginning

"Ye sons of old Killie assembled by Willie
    To follow the noble vocation,
Your thrifty old mother has scarce such another
    To sit in that honoured station.
I've little to say, but only to pray,
As praying's the *ton* of your fashion;
A prayer from the must you well may excuse,
'Tis seldom her favourite passion."

was produced at a festival of the Kilmarnock Lodge, Willie aforesaid being Brother William Parker, the Worshipful Master.

I must not weary you with too many of these snatches of Masonic light from our immortal brother, but it would be impossible to omit the one jewel of jewels of song which he sang, or chanted rather than sang, to the tune of "Good night, and joy be wi' you a'," at the meeting of Lodge St James, Tarbolton, at the moment when his little box of luggage was on its way to Greenock, and he, very soon as he believed, was bound to follow it. We can picture to ourselves the Lodge, Major-General James Montgomery, W.M., in the chair; the Wardens in place; the brethren round the board, and the Depute Master, heart-broken, thinking it the last song he shall ever compose in dear old Scotland. We may picture the meeting, but the emotion of that moment can be but a faint expression.

"Adieu! a heart-warm fond adieu!
    Dear bothers of the mystic tie!
Ye favour'd, ye enlighten'd few,
    Companions of my social joy.
Though I to foreign lands must hie,
    Pursuing fortune's slidd'ry ba'.
With melting heart, and brimful eye,
    I'll mind you still, though far awa'.

Oft have I met your social band,
    And spent the cheerful festive night;
Oft, honoured with supreme command,
    Presided o'er the sons of light,
And by that hieroglyphic bright,
    Which none but craftsmen ever saw!
Strong memory on my heart shall write,
    Those happy scenes when far awa'!

May freedom, harmony, and love,
    Unite you in the grand design,
Beneath the omniscient eye above,
    The glorious Architect divine!
That you may keep the unerring line,
    Still rising by the plummet's law,
Till order bright completely shine
    Shall be my prayer when far awa'.
And you farewell! whose merits claim
    Justly that highest badge to wear.
Heaven bless your honoured noble name
    To Masonry and Scotia dear.
A last request permit me here,
    When yearly ye assemble a',
One round – I ask it with a tear –
    To him, the Bard, that's far awa'."

The tear was quenched; in pursuing "fortune's slidd'ry ba" the poet was led to Edina instead of Jamaica, yet even this not without one sorrow, one tear; for on the very day he entered the beautiful city to be for a flicker her hero of ploughmen, William Wallace, Grand Master of Scotland, "To Masonry and Scotia dear", ascended to the Grand Lodge above.[17]

I pass to the last fragment of my discourse, namely, the tendency and tenure of the genius of Robert Burns as a Masonic poet. With the deepest admiration for a poet whose words have been familiar to me and whose sentiments have touched my heart from the earliest days of my recollection, I am not blind to his sins of emotion. I know his faults. But in all the poet said, and, I believe, thought about the principles of Masonry, he kept by the unerring line, as if indeed the eye omniscient were upon him; and as if in pure Masonry, in its tenets, it symbolisms, and, in the best sense, its practices, there is a secret spell on the mind and heart, in which the mind and heart must live and move and have its being.

The best idea of Masonry on these foundations found its noblest utterance, from our poet brother, in his peroration to St John's Lodge, Kilmarnock.

"Ye powers who preside o'er the wind and the tide,
    Who marked out each element's border;
Who founded this frame with beneficent aim,
    Whose sovereign statute is order.

Within this dear mansion may wayward contention
Or withering envy ne'er enter;
May secrecy round be the mystical bound,
And brotherly love be the centre."

This lecture was first read as a paper at Quatuor Coronati Lodge No. 2076, London, on 4 March 1892. It is a tradition of the lodge that the Worshipful Master calls for comments from the brethren and these are reproduced below.

BRO. ROBERT F. GOULD felt that there could be little to say, except to express his pleasure, and he was sure he might add the pleasure of all the brethren present, at the treat which Bro. Richardson had afforded them. He would, however, in passing, make one remark as to the supposed and so often alleged laureateship of the Canongate Kilwinning Lodge. There was nothing to show that such a title had ever been conferred upon the poet until after his death, and it certainly was in no way borne out by the minutes of the Lodge. He begged to move a vote of thanks to Brother Richardson.

This was seconded by BRO. WESTCOTT, and supported by BRO. CHAMBERLIN, himself a member of the Canongate Kilwinning, and after a few remarks from the Chair, carried by acclamation.

ADDENDUM

Having been requested to make a few remarks on the eloquent prelection which our talented Brother Dr Richardson has delivered on "the Masonic Genius of Robert Burns", I feel I cannot allow the opportunity to pass without expressing in the first place my warm thanks to him for his very interesting sketch of the Masonic career of Scotia's Bard, and in the second place without subjecting some of his remarks to a measure of criticism. But before doing so I would add my commendations to those of the other brethren, and must congratulate the learned doctor upon the admirable apothegm he has given us in his exordium, viz., "Orders are composed of men born to aptitudes befitting the order", which is, I think a very happy and true rendering of the axiom previously formulated, that "In an order or fraternity like Masonry there is a true, a deep, and subtle genius which holds it together: and that the Order may be held together there must be, in a greater or lesser degree, the same kind of genius in every individual member", from which he deduces the truth that "Masonry was akin to Burns' native genius, it was to him that touch of nature which makes all akin." It was this "one touch of nature", this inborn feeling or perception of the universality of the brotherhood of man so frequently expressed in his works, which constituted his Masonic genius. For instance, we have in the following lines, which are most characteristic of the writer, the fundamental principle or spirit of Masonry:

"A' ye whom social pleasure charms,
Whose heart the tide of kindness warms,
Wha hold your being on the terms,
　'Each aid the others,'
Come to my bowl, come to my arms,
　My friends, my BROTHERS."

And again in the manly lines of the song beginning "Is there for honest poverty, wha hangs his head and a' that," this feeling finds expression in the noble aspiration:

"Then let us pray that come it may –
    As come it will for a' that –
That sense and worth o'er a' the earth
    May bear the gree, and a' that,
For a' that, and a' that
    It's comin' yet for a' that,
That man to man, the warld o'er,
    Shall brithers be for a' that."

Herein lies the great secret of Burns' universal popularity: not only his love of nature, which is a common attribute of all poets, but by his intense love of human nature, he was endowed with a deeper sympathy with humanity enabling him to strike a chord in all our hearts which vibrates in unison with that which thrilled his own, deepening our sympathies towards our fellow men and enlarging our hearts in universal love. This is, without doubt, the keystone of the great arch of Burns' Masonic genius.

Our poet's family name, as Brother Richardson observes, was not always Burns but was originally Burness, and it may interest the brethren on 25 May 1786, he announced to the brethren of the Lodge at Tarbolton that he intended assuming in future the shorter name of Burns, and he accordingly signed the minutes that evening for the first time by the now familiar and world-famous name of Robert Burns. Brother Richardson informs us of his regular attendance in the Lodge, and mentions that he attended to his duties nine times in the year 1785 and the same number of times in 1786, and we find the minute book bearing ample and valuable testimony as to his assiduity as a Mason, for page after page is filled with his hand writing and his autograph as Depute Master, thus making the little volume of this out-of-the-way Lodge more valuable than the records of the most ancient Lodge in the world.

We come now to Burns' appearance in Edinburgh amongst the brethren there, and here I would take objection to the statement that on 1 March 1787, Bro. Alexander Fergusson of Craigdarrock, the Master of Lodge Canongate Kilwinning, "dignified him as Poet Laureate of the Brotherhood, and assigned him a special poet's throne". There is nothing to warrant this assertion, which has been frequently made and as frequently contradicted, but the idea is a popular one and forms the subject of a well-known picture by the late Bro. Stewart Watson which has done much to perpetuate the fallacy. As Bro. Richardson says, Burns was assumed a member of Lodge Canongate Kilwinning on 1 February 1787, the minutes of the meeting being in the following terms: "The Right Worshipful Master, having observed that Brother Burns was at present in the Lodge, who is well known as a great Poetic Writer, and for a late publication of his Works, which have been universally commended, and submitted that he should be assumed a Member of this Lodge, which was unanimously agreed to, and he was assumed accordingly", but the minutes contain no reference to his having been laureated by the Lodge. Brother D. Murray Lyon, in his well-known History, says, "The 1 March 1787, is men-

107

tioned by Masonic writers as the date of the scene which has been portrayed by the artist. But neither the minutes of that date, nor of any other during Burns' lifetime contain any record whatever of the existence of such an office as Laureate of the Lodge or of that distinction being conferred on Burns. The first mention in Canongate Kilwinning minutes of this office having been held by the Poet is found under date 9 February 1815, when the Lodge resolved to open a subscription among its members to aid in the erection of a "Mausoleum to the memory of Robert Burns, who was a member and Poet Laureate of this Lodge'," a very evident afterthought which is repeated in the minute of 9 June 1815, and again in that of 16 January 1835, which chronicles the appointment of Brother James Hogg, the "Ettrick shepherd", to the "honorary office of Poet Laureate of the Lodge, which had been 'in abeyance since the death of the immortal Brother Robert Burns'."

Dr Richardson, like a skilful physician, delicately touches a tender spot, when he says he knows our poet's faults and is "not blind to his sins of emotion". Some persons there are who have not this delicacy, and I am sorry to say there are many who do not deal so gently or kindly with our brother's memory as he would have done himself in the case of an erring brother, for does he not counsel us to do so in these well-known lines?

"Then gently scan your brother man,
    Still gentler sister woman;
Though they may gang a kennin' wrang
    To step aside is human;
One point must still be greatly dark,
    The moving *Why* they do it,
And just as lamely can ye mark
    How far, perhaps, they rue it.

Who made the heart, 'tis He alone,
    Decidedly can try us,
He knows each chord – its various tone,
    Each spring – its various bias;
Then at the balance let's be mute,
    We never can adjust it;
What's done we partly may compute,
    But know not what's resisted."

Let us exercise towards his memory then that charity which we, as Masons, profess to admire and cultivate, and leave, as he himself would have us leave, the judgment of our actions to the Maker of the heart. Like Dr Richardson I, too, from my earliest years have been acquainted with the works of the poet, and have studied them, and sighed over the short sad story of his life in my maturer years, and the more I study the more I appreciate "the God-made King", and thank the Giver of all good who

"– sent his singers upon earth,
With songs of sadness and of mirth,
That they might reach the hearts of men,
And bring them back to heaven again."

108

and not the least among them "To charm, to strengthen, and to teach", is our poet brother, Robert Burns.

One more point and I have done, and sorry am I to have occasion to note this point; it is in reference to a certain obnoxious volume of doggerel which is palmed upon an inconsiderate world as Burns' "Merry Muses". I would humbly suggest that the mere fact that some of the contents of the book are in the handwriting of Allan Cunningham is no conclusive proof that Burns ever wrote a single line of it, because Allan Cunningham was not acquainted with Burns, he was not the poet's friend; he was a boy of a little over ten years of age when the poet died, and it is not likely that Burns would contract a friendship with a youth of that age, or confide to him songs of such a nature that the rare volume must needs be concealed as a forbidden book to the eyes of childhood. No! a thousand times no! I have seen and read the filthy volume, and there is not one redeeming point in it. One can tolerate smut when it is classical or witty, as in the *Decameron* and some of our ancient masters, but when it is unaccompanied by wit or cleverness or sense or reason it is intolerable: and the halting lines, the spurious rhymes, and contemptible stuff contained in this volume stamp it as the offspring, not of a genius like Burns, but of some grovelling prurient incestuous mind or minds. Like Thomas, I doubt and will not believe until I have ample proof, and not till I see the lines in his own holograph, or with his name adhibited in his well-known hand will I be convinced that our much loved poet, and much maligned by the "unco' guid", ever penned these foul effusions. The songs of our country were dross and worse until the advent of Burns; it was he who, by the refining power of his divine gift, turned them into pure gold, and gave them a free unsullied gift to his countrymen, and I cannot entertain in my own mind for a single moment that he, who had done so much towards purifying the literature of his country, would ever leave it such a degrading legacy as the "Merry Muses", which I maintain is frequently falsely and calumniously, but I trust thoughtlessly, ascribed to him. We know but too well that there are stains and splashes on his regal robes, but even in his cups he never degraded his high office, he never deliberately doffed and dragged those robes through the mire. What says his centenary poet?

> "Though he may yield
>   Hard-pressed, and wounded fall
> Forsaken on the field;
>   His regal vestments soiled;
> His crown of half its jewels spoiled;
>   He is a king for all."

I am sorry that I am compelled to speak so strongly, but I feel strongly, and think that as this paper has been devoted to the "Masonic Genius of Burns", it is a fit and proper place to enter once for all a protest against the calumny which so often ascribes this foul doggerel to the Bard of Scotland. In conclusion, I feel that we all owe Bro. Dr. Richardson a deep debt of gratitude for his admirable and eloquent address upon "The Masonic Genius of Robert Burns" – W. FRED VERNON.

EDITOR'S FOOTNOTES TO CHAPTER THIRTEEN

1. Readers should re-read Part I for an accurate account of the St James/St David story.
2. Kirkoswald is half a mile from the fishing port of Maidens.
3. A misleading description. Gilbert did not accompany Robert to the port at Irvine.
4. Mossgiel is nearer Mauchline than it is Tarbolton.
5. The Bachelors' Club and its members were most respectable and reputable.
6. Not quite accurate.
7. This meeting of the Lodge was held in Mauchline.
8. More probably he resided with his aunt, Jean Brown, a sister of his mother and wife of James Allan at Old Rome (or Old Room Foord) midway between Kilmarnock and Irvine.
9. A harsh description.
10. A somewhat inaccurate description.
11. A letter from Dr. Blacklock reached him through the Rev. G. Lawrie, Minister of Loudoun, Newmilns.
12. Vide the "Canongate Controversy" Chapter 3 of Part III.
13. "Intemperance" could be qualified by a reference to other symptoms of his illness.
14. "Informal Lodge" is an unfortunate description.
15. Wilson did not accompany Burns, even part of the way, home.
16. This is not so. Wilson remained in the village for several years after the incident.
17. The comment is true but misleading. The description refers to the Master of Lodge St James.

This was a most erudite treatise, unfortunately spoiled by too many factual errors. It was all too obvious Brother Richardson was perpetuating stories without verifying them. There was also the hint, too, that he was supporting the "Currie-Heron" views of the poet's indiscretions. Brother Fred W. Vernon's Addendum was a welcome "corrective".

Chapter Fourteen

Lecture Three

ROBERT BURNS AS A FREEMASON

A Lecture delivered to the Edinburgh Masters' and Past Masters' Association, on 13 October 1916, by WILLIAM LAWSON, PM, Lodge St David, Edinburgh, No. 36.

As nearly every Scottish freemason knows, Robert Burns, "Caledonia's Bard", was made a member of the "Craft" in a Lodge in Tarbolton, a village which, for at least eight years, had meagrely supported two separate Lodges, but which, just nine days previous to the Poet's initiation, had witnessed the junction of these Lodges, under the name "St David", and the number 174. It is also generally known that Burns was a member of several Lodges in Ayrshire previous to his advent in Edinburgh; that during his visits to the city his name appears once in the minutes of a Metropolitan Lodge; that at Eyemouth he became a Royal Arch mason, and that in Dumfries he ended his Masonic career as a member of Lodge St Andrew, No. 179.

Considered generally, his personality, his genius, and his work, mark Burns as one of the brightest figures that have ever adorned the roll of the Scottish Masonic Brotherhood. Yet, from a purely Masonic point of view, it cannot be said that he was either a great or a prominent Freemason. The masonic interests in his life were certainly very conspicuous, and quite a number of essays have been written dealing specially with this subject. There are beside, a host of biographies, in which his Masonic activities are more or less fully commented on and considered. Under these circumstances, and at this date, one may hardly hope to produce anything of moment that is new, but can only endeavour, in the time at our disposal, to fill in the facts in detail of the Poet's honourable and enthusiastic membership of our "Ancient Order".

It will certainly help us to an understanding of our subject if, at the outset, we briefly review the history of the two Lodges in that little silk-weaving Ayrshire village. Without doing so, it will be more than difficult to follow or appreciate why, or how, Burns joined St David, and spent most of his Masonic life in service at the altar of Lodge St James, Tarbolton, Kilwinning.

The first Masonic Lodge in Tarbolton was "Tarbolton Kilwinning", erected by Charter from the Mother Lodge of Kilwinning on 17 May 1771. The first list of Officers of the new Lodge include Alexander Montgomerie of Coilsfield, as Grand Master, John Hood, as Deputy Master, and six others, but there is no mention of either a Secretary or a Treasurer.

The Lodge itself passed twenty-one "Rules", some of which are very quaintly expressed – evidently they are after some ancient model. To these original rules there are two additions of a later date, one referring to "Squairsmen" and another which, since it is signed by the Poet, may be quoted.

"7th Dec. 1785.
"The Lodge thought proper to commit to writing that old Regulation. That whoever stands as Master, shall be bound at the entery of a new Member, for that Member's dues, if the money is not paid or Security such as the Lodge shall approve of given."

This old Regulation is written by "Dr Hornbook", and is signed Robt. Burness.

In the year 1773 a secession of Brethren took place, when Sir Thomas Wallace, Bart., and nineteen others applied to the Grand Lodge of Scotland for a Charter. This Charter, No. 174 (present number 133) was granted on 26 February 1773, and is signed by Patrick, Earl of Dumfries, Grand Master, and five others. The first existing minute states:-

> "1773. Feby. 26 was the day of the Charter of St David's Lodge being granted in faiver of Sir Thos. Walles Bart.," etc. etc.

Perhaps the minute of March 1774 will explain several things, particularly in regard to the existing Minute Book.

> "This was the day that the Lodge was consecraited and received their instructions from Thos Bestin" (assisted by five others be it said) "from Killmarnock St Andrews Lodge No 166, who installed for Deputy Master, John Mitchel. . . ."

A complete list of Office-Bearers follows, and the minute concludes:

> ". . . As nothing pertickler passed from March 15, 1774 to March 1st 1775 the Sederants are left in the Old Book."

The "pertickler" thing that "passed" on the latter date was an election of Office-Bearers, when twenty members were present. 28 June following being the "Day of the Perseshen", (twenty-two members and five visitors, being present), the minute again finishes with the phrase, "As nothing pertickler passed from 1 Mar. 1777 to 3 Jan. 1778 the Sederunts are left in the Old Book". Evidently the "Perseshen" is the only "pertickler" business between 1776 and 1778, but what we wish specially to note is, that the present Minute Book is not the "Old Book", whatever that may suggest.

In 1774 Tarbolton Kilwinning itself applied to Grand Lodge for a Charter, which on 27 May was granted with the title "St James Tarbolton Kilwinning", and the number 178 (now 135). The Grand Master of Scotland was "Prince John, Duke of Atholl". He did not sign the Charter, but it is signed by six Grand Officers, including James Boswell, S.G.W., and Harry Erskine, J.G.W., both of whom were afterwards associated with the Poet. Every Brother present on 24 June 1774, when this Charter was read to the Lodge, signed his name after a copy of it in the Minute Book, into which it has been carefully engrossed. There is a procession to Church, a sermon by the parish minister, Mr Patrick Wodrow – "Himself a member", a return procession, and an election of Office-Bearers.

James Montgomerie now being Master, and Hood still Deputy, we have James Manson, the Innkeeper, appearing for the first time in office as Treasurer.

Between this date, 1774, and 1781, there were three Grand Masters, i.e. nominal heads of the Lodge, the Deputy Master being generally in "supreme command". These Grand Masters were John Hamilton of Sundrum, Alexander Montgomerie of Coilsfield, and Mungo Smith, Esq., of Drongan.

This brings us to the union of the two Lodges, and with that, the advent of Burns into Freemasonry. For any reference to the joining of the two Tarbolton Lodges on 25 June 1781, we search the book of Lodge St James in vain. It is not until nearly twelve months after the event that the subject is mentioned. In Lodge

Manson's Inn in 1906

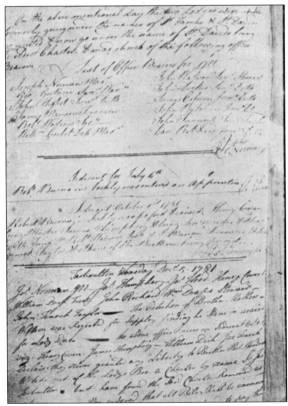

Minute of Initiation in Lodge St David Tarbolton

113

St David minutes it is different, for there we find that on 6 December 1780, "It was proposed to make a union with Tarbolton Lodge", and on 6 June 1781 we have this:

". . . and have considered on Our Offers to St James Lodge Respecting a Juncten on 24; allso their answer and finds by a majority of Votes that both Lodges may Unite on Terms offered and exchanged this day."

Both the quoted minutes are signed "James Samson, Master."
The minute recording the actual union is in these terms:-

"Sederant for June 25th 1788.
". . . On the above mentioned day the two Lodges formerly going under the names of St James and St David were united and brought under the name of St Davids, being the oldest Charter, and made choice of the following Office Bearers."

Here follows a list of ten office-bearers, the positions being filled by a division of honours between the two Lodges, as far down as Deputy Master, who follows the Secretary, thereafter each office has two brethren in it, one from each Lodge, thus there is a "Senior Taylor", and a "Junior Ditto".

This minute is signed "Joph Norman, M." Attention may be called to the why and wherefor of the united body being called St David. ". . . being the oldest charter", is the ungrammatical reason given, and must refer to the Grand Lodge Charters only.

Norman, who signs, had joined St David in 1776, and was a Past Master, but seems to have been chosen at the last moment as the man best capable of carrying the Lodges through this crisis in their histories. The Secretary was Brother Robert Wodrow, of whom there will be more to say later.

Nine days after the joining of the Lodges we have one of the shortest minutes in the book, it read thus:

"Sederant for July 4th
"Robt Burns in Lochly" (i.e. Lochlee) was entered an Apprentice
Joph Norman, M. "

With so poor a heralding our hero steps upon the stage. Burns' entry-money was 12/6d, and it was paid on this date, i.e., at his initiation.

Almost immediately after this Burns went to Irvine, on a promising, but ultimately "ill starred" venture. On 1 October, having presumably walked the twelve miles from Irvine to Tarbolton, we find Burns being "passed and raised". The event is recorded thus:

"Sederant October 1st 1781.
{Robert Burns in Lochly was passed and raised Henry Cowan being Master, James Humphrey" (the *"bleth'rin bitch"*) "Senr Warden and Alexr Smith Junr Do. Robert Wodrow Secy and Jas Manson Treasurer and John Tannock Taylor and others of the Brethren being present.
Joph Norman, M. "

No mention is made anywhere before 1784 as to the place where either Lodge held its meetings, but from the careful consideration of various incidents mentioned here and there throughout the minute books, one is driven to the conclusion that

114

Burns was *not* made a Freemason in Manson's Inn, as is generally stated and believed. In support of this conclusion the following facts may be mentioned:

Lodge St James did not meet in Manson's until June 1784 (see minute), so that, if the united Lodge met on 4 July 1781, in St James' meeting place, Burns was certainly not made a Freemason in Manson's. On the other hand, if the initiation meeting was held – as is likely – in the Lodge-room of St David, these points are to be considered:-

1st. Except for the brief period of the junction of the Lodges, Manson was never in any way associated with Lodge St David, but had been continuously Treasurer of St James since 1774.

2nd. In the years referred to, a "Public House" stood on the site of the present Post Office, kept, as we are informed, by John Richard. This Richard was a prominent member of Lodge St David, had been Steward for several years, and had charge of the Charter Chest, and other property of the Lodge, as the minutes testify. It is surely reasonable to suppose that if St David's meeting place was associated with an inn, it was John Richard's rather than James Manson's.

3rd. In a minute of Lodge St David, previous to 1781, it is stated that the procession of the Lodge, after its annual church service, returned to the hall. At that date there was only one place in Tarbolton which could, by any stretch of imagination, be called a "Hall". It was the room in which the Bachelor Club held its meetings, and was next door to John Richard's "Public House"; indeed the stair by which this hall was reached came down to within a yard or two of Richard's back door.

A consideration of these facts, among others, encourage the belief that "Burns" was made in the Bachelor Club room, and that the Manson story has arisen from the fact that during the whole term of Burns as Deputy Master of Lodge St James, that Lodge held its meetings in Manson's Inn.

At the next meeting (Dec. '81) we find that the elected Secretary, Bro. Robert Woodrow, had "abstracted" the Books and Charters of Lodge St James from the "Charter Chest" of St David, and we have the beginning of a very pretty quarrel, and the end of the "Junchen". Wodrow, a son of the manse, had never liked the subordination of his mother Lodge, St James, and now, backed by young Captain James Montgomerie, he refused to surrender the Books and Charters which he had removed – they call it abstracted – from the possession of Lodge St David. That Lodge finally took proceedings against him in the Sheriff Court at Ayr. The Sheriff Substitute's "Interlocketer" (Lodge records) was in effect. "As the junction had been voluntary there was nothing to present a voluntary seperation." St David appealed to William Wallace, Sheriff Depute, who in his turn declared that this was not a case for the "cevall courts" (Lodge spelling), but should be referred to Grand Lodge. Referred it was, and Grand Committee ordered restoration of the documents. Wodrow still remained defiant, and so it is recorded in St James' Book.

"Tarbolton, 17th June 1782.
"St James Lodge met upon the same footing as it was before the junction.
James Montgomerie

Gr. Mr. for the night."

And thus the junction was a thing of the past.

From his passing and raising in 1781, until after the death of his father in 1784, there is no mention of Burns as a Mason. Whether he attended the meetings of either Lodge, or, if, so, which between October '81 and July '84, we have no means of clearly knowing, but the inference is that he attended Lodge St James, for in the latter month we find him elected as Depute Master of that Lodge.

The Minute Book of Lodge St James during '82 and '83 contains little to interest us. In August 1782 John Wilson, the Schoolmaster – afterwards immortalised by the Poet as "Dr Hornbook" – became Secretary. The next item

Burns' Chairs Tarbolton. D. M. G.

The Candlesticks used in Burns' time at Tarbolton, still used by the Lodge.

Burns' Jewel, Tarbolton.

Burns' Mallet, Tarbolton.

of interest is dated 30 June 1784, when St James Lodge removed "From its present meeting place of James Manson's". Then, at the first meeting in "Manson's", Robert Burns is elected Deputy Master, as already stated. In this office Burns remained until July 1788. During these years he had trouble with the Armours, published his poems, visited Edinburgh twice, took several tours, and had begun the rebuilding of Ellisland. He generally presided at the meetings, and signed many of the minutes. Until 25 May 1786 he spelt his name Burness, but strangely enough, it is Burns on the roll of members, where it is accompanied by his Mark. Only on three known occasions previous to 1786, Burns had spelt his name as we now do – and as everyone

but he and his brother Gilbert did then, viz.:– once in a letter to Thomas Orr, dated 17 November, 1782, a second time in his second "Epistle to J. Lapraik", where the "feet" of his metre requires one syllable, and lastly in "The Inventory", where it is required to rhyme with "concerns".

Perhaps at this point some reference may be made to another Mark, which the Poet inscribed in one of the volumes of the Bible he exchanged with his still somewhat elusive Highland Mary.* There is no record of any Mark meeting at which Burns could have received, or registered a Mark, and it is generally supposed that, like many others of his day, he adopted one. He is known to have used it only on the two occasions mentioned.

Nothing worthy of note occurs in Lodge St James during Burns' first year of office. On 1 June 1785 it is recorded that "The Lodge unanimously thanked the Grand Master (i.e., Captain Montgomerie) for his trouble in recovering their colours for some time illegally retained by the Lodge of St David." Frankly, he (Montgomerie) and Wodrow had recovered them by a process which to-day would

*The Bible Mark has been generally taken to be different from that in the Lodge, but our Editor suggests that it is the same Mark written perpendicularly and partly obliterated, as some other parts of the writing in the volumes are. We entirely agree.

be called theft. The following letter from Robert Andrew, Treasurer of St David, to the R.W.M., is both entertaining and instructive.

"Tarbolton 29th May 1785."
"Sir
This is to inform you that last night Captn James Montgomery with his Collig Robt Widrow came to John Richards bout Eight oclock and called for two Gills of punch and sent John Richard to James Mansons for Gavin Hamilton and the time he was out the two for said went to the room where the Charter Chest stands and Broke it up and Carried of the flag with what other things we do not know as John Richard got Mr Hamilton as a wittness that they had done it and made him Seal up the Chest until further enquiry be made after their Crime Capt James owned before John Richard, Mr Hamilton and Robt Wodrow that he had done it and that it was his own and he would stand on the head of what he had done."

It is only fair to Capt. Montgomery to explain that when Lodge St David took action in the Sheriff Court against Robert Wodrow he (the Captain) had taken a Counter action against St David for the restoration of Lodge St James' effects, and had received a decree in his favour. This may account for the phrase "illegally retained" in the St James minute, and explains why they thanked their Master for upholding a judgment by an illegal act. On 2 August a deputation of the Lodge to "Machlin" is mentioned for the first time. Visits to Mauchline became quite common after this. It was on such a visit that Gilbert Burns was entered, passed and raised – presumably by his brother – though the fee was not paid until the Lodge meeting in Tarbolton immediately following. On 18 August, Burns is ordered to procure a new "Master Cloth". In September a new Compass and Square were procured.

The really interesting thing of this year is the production of "Death and Dr. Hornbook". It was known in Tarbolton in '85. It is said to have been composed after a Lodge meeting, and surely never was penned a happier description of the possible condition of a D.M. after a convivial meeting, than that contained in the third and two following verses of this "Brotherly" satire. It has been said that the satire was too cutting for Wilson, and that he was driven from the village. Well! that may be so, but he was certainly a long time "a-driving", for he remained Secretary for some years, and was Session Clerk until 1793. He signed minutes of the Lodge as D.M., *pro tempore,* in April 1786, and again in June '88.

The year 1786 is in many respects the most interesting year of Burns' life. It was a broken and harassing year, a year of trouble and uncertainty, but the year of his triumph also. He had missed only one meeting of the Lodge, from the date of his election as D.M. until April of this year. About this time it will be remembered that Armour had flatly refused to acknowledge "Jean" as wife of the Poet, and Burns was horribly upset. His letter to John Arnot in April voices a profound depression, which he refers to in June to David Brice thus " . . . I have tried often to forget her (i.e., Jean); I have run into all kinds of dissipation and riot, mason meetings, drinking-matches and other mischief, to drive her out of my head, but all in vain." To get into "mischief" Burns seems to have moved about the country-side from place to place. On 27 March we find him a visitor at Gavin Hamilton's Lodge, at Newmilns, and we have the following record:

"27th March, Loudon Kilwinning, Newmilns.
"Much to the satisfaction of the Lodge, Mr Robert Burns, Mossgiel, Mauchline, introduced by the Right Worshiful, was admitted a member of this Lodge."

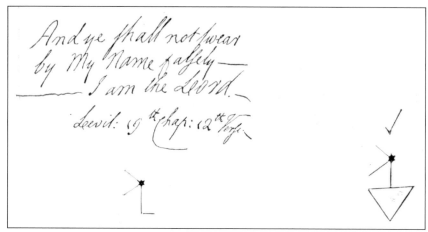

Burns' Inscription on Highland Mary's Bible (Vol. 1).

Mossgiel

Gavin Hamilton was the Right Worshipful referred to. The minute goes on to relate that a Mr John Hunter – a member of St Peters, Galston – was also admitted on payment of five shillings, and the minute concludes, "John Morton, merchant in Newmilns is Answerable for Mr Robert Burns' admission Money." Poor Burns!

The next appearance of Burns in St James's, was at the second meeting in May, when Montgomerie himself presided and signed. On 25 May, we find the Poet in the chair, and signing for the first time with his new version of the previous name "Burness". Eleven days before this Burns (we are told by himself) had parted from Highland Mary who, it is said, had gone home to prepare for marriage with the Bard. On 12 June, Burns settled to go to Jamaica. The farm (Mossgiel) had proved a failure, and the outlook on life was now gloomy and almost hopeless. On 16 June

118

Diploma of Lodge St David, Tarbolton

he was re-elected Depute Master. Wilson is still Secretary, and Gilbert goes into office as Junior Warden.

Through the advice of some of his Masonic friends, Hamilton, Ballantine, Aiken and Goldie, Burns – having found a "Brother" in Kilmarnock willing to publish for him – had decided to venture into print, and was about this time living at Old Rome, and seeing his work through the press. The famous book, published on 31 July 1786, was an immediate and assured success. Strangely enough, so far as we can see, it contains no single verse that had been written before its author became a Freemason. With the profits of the publication, £20, in his pocket – and an apparently fine disregard for Mary – Burns prepared to sail for the West Indies in August. Something intervened, and September was spoken of as the sailing month. September, however, provided promise of a different harvest, for the "Book" had pleased not only the general public, but had also found favour with the critics. An unexpected letter

Ellisland

119

from Edinburgh, from one of "A sort of Critics for whose applause I had not dared to hope", suggested to the Poet the publication of a second and larger edition of the Poems, to be printed in Edinburgh. Wilson, his original publisher, was shy of a second venture, and Ballantine of Ayr, while offering to guarantee the cost of the paper for a new edition, if published in Kilmarnock, strongly urged Burns to make Edinburgh the venue of any future publication. The letter from Dr Blacklock, Edinburgh, to his friend the Revd George Lawrie of Loudoun, urging the publication of a second edition, is dated 4 September, but did not reach the Poet's hands for some weeks. Although Burns did not immediately act upon Blacklock's suggestion, its effect, together with the advice of Ballantine and others, was to induce the Poet to postpone consideration of his departure for Jamaica.

Burns seems to have been particularly well known to the Masonic fraternity in and about Kilmarnock, and to have been on terms of intimacy with many of the brethren of Lodge St John Kilwinning, No. 24 (now 22). This Lodge had been founded mainly by the efforts of the ill-fated Lord Kilmarnock, and dates from 1734. It came under Grand Lodge of Scotland in April 1737. The minute of a meeting of this Lodge dated 26 October 1786 reads thus:

> "Present the Right Worshipful Master, Deputy Master, and several brethren, when John Galt, farmer, in Cressland, was upon his petition made an entered apprentice; At same time Robert Burns, poet, from Mauchline, a member of St James's, Tarbolton, was made an honorary member of this Lodge.
>
> Will Parker."

This is Burns' first honorary membership, and for the first time masonically he is designated "Poet".

On 10 November Burns presided in the Lodge at Tarbolton, and about a fortnight later set out for Edinburgh. On the evening of 28 November he arrived in the city. He came neither as a ploughman nor as a Freemason, but as a Poet, and as a Poet he was received.

This fact is one it is important for us to remember, for it has been seriously stated that, but for the Masons in Edinburgh, Burns might never have become famous. Well! we demur. It is everywhere admitted that Burns was largely helped and assisted in many ways by the Masonic friendships he established and enjoyed during his first visit to "Edina, Scotia's darling seat", but to suggest, in effect, that the Masonic Brotherhood in Edinburgh *made* Burns is to assume too much. Burns had already "arrived", as we say to-day. "The Kilmarnock Edition" had been published, and its author's fame and position were already assured.

Whether his night at Covington or his two days in the saddle had upset him cannot be said, but we are told that Burns spent his first day in town in Richmond's bed. So far as we know there was not a man in Edinburgh whom Burns had previously met as a "Brother", indeed there seem to have been only three persons in the City with whom Burns had previously spoken: Richmond, his Mauchline friend, James Dalrymple of Orangefield, to whom he had been introduced by Ballantine at Ayr, and Professor Dougald Stewart, with whom Burns had dined in the previous month.

Sixty years after the alleged event, it was stated that Burns attended a meeting of Lodge Canongate Kilwinning, on 7 December. That may be so, but, as neither a traditional nor a recorded support can be given for the statement, its truth has been the subject of suspicion. Still more suspicious is the assertion that after

120

that meeting – mark you *after* the meeting – Burns wrote a letter to Gavin Hamilton, telling him of the sale of certain Ayrshire farms – Mossgiel amongst them – and commenting on "My own affairs", he told how "My Lord Glencairn and the Dene of Faculty have taken me under their wing", also that in Mr Dalrymple of Orangefield he had found what "Solomon emphatically calls, a friend that sticketh closer than a brother". It is much more likely that this letter had been written on 5 or 6 December – the sale took place on 5 December – and that it is dated on the day of its despatch. Post dating was a practice not unusual with the Poet.

The first recorded visit to a Lodge in Edinburgh is in Burns' own hand, in a letter to Mr Ballantine, dated 14 January. Here again, the date does not agree with the "yester-night" of the letter, for the meeting was held on the twelfth. The meeting referred to by Burns was the annual visit of the Grand Lodge of Scotland to Lodge Edinburgh St Andrew. The Hon. Francis Charteris, Grand Master, took occasion to propose from the chair a toast to "Caledonia, and Caledonia's Bard, Brother Burns", and the Poet relates that, although taken by surprise, "I made the best return in my power", and that from remarks overheard at the close of his speech, his audience thought he had acquitted himself "Very well indeed".

At a meeting of Canongate Kilwinning, on 1 February 1787, we have the only minuted record of Burns' presence in a City Lodge. The second and concluding paragraph of this minute relates that the Lodge honoured the Poet – and, as it has proved, honoured themselves also – thus:

"The Right Worshipful Master having observed that Bro. Burns was at present in the Lodge who is well known as a great Poetic Writer and for a late publication of his Works which have been universally Commended. And Submitted that he should be assumed a member of this Lodge which was unanimously agreed to and he was assumed accordingly."

This brings us to the so-called "Inauguration Meeting", and the appointment of Burns as Poet Laureate of Lodge Canongate Kilwinning. A comparatively recent controversy over the authenticity of the statement that Burns ever was so appointed has put this question beyond mere acceptance on the strength of the assertions of either side, and has created a very argumentative position. The arguments, *pro.* and *con.*, are much too long for us to consider here and now, and we can simply offer an opinion – an opinion arrived at after a careful consideration of all the available testimony. Our opinion then is that Burns was undoubtedly known and recognised by his contemporary members as Poet Laureate of Lodge Canongate Kilwinning.* There is a well established and continuous testimony confirming this; on the other hand, there is not even a reasonable tradition as to any inauguration, and we do not believe it took place. The well known picture by Brother Stewart Watson was not conceived or executed until 1845. It is purely imaginary, and has no value as a witness. It bears on its face refutation of its truth, for it contains portraits of men who were not Freemasons, one of whom did not meet Burns until 1789, two years after the date of this meeting.

We should have liked to say something as to the coldness and indifference with which Burns – the man, rather than the Poet, this time – was received on his second

* In this connection it may be interesting to quote the following letter by the late Grand Secretary, Brother D. Murray Lyon to the Lodge, and entered in the minutes, in which he says, "The Poet Burns was a member, and was elected Poet Laureate of Lodge Canongate Kilwinning, to which many of his friends belonged. He was not installed as represented by Brother Stewart Watson's picture, but there may have been some ceremony on the occasion. Probably there was. There is evidence for it." *ED.*

visit to Edinburgh. Even on this visit the friends who clung to him were for the most part Masons, but of "lesser degree". This must be left, for it is time for our visit to Eyemouth.

On 5 May 1787, Burns set out in company with his friend, Robert Ainslie – a Brother of Lodge St Luke – on his first tour. It is known as the "Border Tour", and took him by way of Duns, Coldstream, Kelso, Jedburgh, Bonchester, Selkirk, Innerleithen, back to Duns, and thence to Eyemouth, where he arrived on the eighteenth of the month. Here the Masonic chain is again linked up, for on Sunday 19 May he was exalted as a Royal Arch Mason. The minute of the meeting on that day is not now in the possession of the Chapter, but is available because it had already appeared in print before it was lost – or stolen. It reads thus:

> *"Eyemouth 19th May 1787.*
> "At a general encampment held this day, the following Brethren were made Royal Arch Masons, namely:- Robert Burns, from Lodge St James, Tarbolton, Ayrshire; and Robert Ainslie from the Lodge of St Luke, Edinburgh, by James Carmichael, William Grieve, Donald Dow, John Clay, Robert Grieve etc., etc. Robert Ainslie paid one guinea admission dues, but, on account of Robert Burns's remarkable poetical genius, the encampment unanimously agreed to admit him *gratis,* and considered themselves honoured by having a man of such shining abilities for one of their companions."

This may have been edited, but it is certainly the best Burns masonic minute ever written.

The ceremony seems to have taken place in a Preceptory Encampment, and an interesting point for us is that three months later, i.e., on 9 August, the Encampment received a Charter from England, constituting it a Royal Arch Chapter. The name of the Chapter was "Land of Cakes", and its number 52. The first principals were the friends Burns met, William Grieve, Z., Robert Grieve, H., and James Carmichael, J. It is now No. 15 on the Scottish Roll.

Twice Burns makes written reference to this degree, once in his journal of the Border Tour where he records the fact of having been "made", and again in a letter to Ainslie on 25 June 1787, written from Arrochar, in which he addresses him as "My Dear Friend and Brother Arch". This is the whole record of Burns' Royal Arch career.

On 9 June Burns arrived quietly back at Mossgiel, and on 19 June was re-elected D.M. in Lodge St James. There is no word of his being present at this meeting, and the minute is unsigned. He presided, however, at a meeting in Mauchline on 25 July. This was his only known attendance at the Lodge in the year 1787, but it was a great occasion.

> "This night the deputation of the Lodge met at Mauchline and entered Brother Alexander Allison of Barmuir an apprentice Likewise admitted Brs Professor Stewart, of Catrine, and Claud Alexander, Esqr. of Ballochmyle, Claud Nielson, Esqr. of Paisley, John Farquhar Gray, Esqr. of Gilmilncroft and Dr George Grierson, Glasgow Honorary Members of this Lodge
>
> Robt. Burns D.M."

Burns returned to Edinburgh on 7 August, and on 23rd of the month wrote the famous letter to St James – still in possession of the Lodge – beginning, "Men and Brethren I am truly sorry it is not in my power to be at your quarterly meeting", and ending with four lines of poetry, which he had previously used in his address to "Ye sons of old Killie". With the exception of two words it is identical with the last four lines of the Kilmarnock poem.

Burns appears to have taken possession at Ellisland on or about 13 June 1788, but the house was in a wretched condition and required re-building. During the months that followed we find him nearly as much at Mauchline, where he and Jean after their marriage had set up house, as at Ellisland. He had been twice present in St James, during May '88, but on 24 June James Findlay (Burns' teacher in excise duties) was elected D.M. under James Dalrymple, of Orangefield, as Master. Burns was in the Chair at a meeting in Mauchline on 21 October, and presided again on 11 November, this being his last appearance in Lodge St James.

During the period from Burns' election as Deputy Master in 1784 until his last meeting in '88, Lodge St James had been convened seventy times. At thirty-three of these meetings Burns had been present – notwithstanding his long terms of absence in 1787 and 1788. He signed twenty-five times as presiding officer and twice in other parts of the book, once at the Old Regulation, and once on the Roll of Members. Thirteen times in all his name is spelt "Burness", once only preceded by the full Christian name Robert; the remaining signatures "Burns" have once the full Robert, once the initial R, but generally the poet uses the familiar contraction Robt. A postscript to the first signed minute is initialled R.B. Strangely enough, the two full names, "Robert Burness" and "Robert Burns", are the first and the last signatures to the minutes of meetings. There are three brief Holograph minutes by Burns.

As we have seen, Burns came to Ellisland in June but it was not until the first week in the December that he found the place fit to receive his wife. Very soon after being thus established on the banks of the Nith we find him acquiring a new Masonic connection, for on 21st December he joined Lodge Dumfries St Andrew, No. 179. There were six Lodges in Dumfries at this time, but the Poet seems to have selected the weakest of them. Perhaps it was the number that attracted him, but he was unfortunate for the Lodge was moribund. It had been Chartered in 1774 by the same Grand Lodge officials as St James. Its first Right Worshipful Master was R. Douglas, Clerk of Customs. At its third meeting Charles Sharp of Hoddom – afterwards P.G.M. of Dumfriesshire – was assumed a member. Here, again, we have quaint rules; e.g. it is an offence to swear or whisper, and a brother who appears "Disguised in Liquor" will be severely punished. The fee was twenty-five shillings, affiliation fee ten shillings, and a brother who had been in good standing for three years with his quarterly dues was, on falling into distress, to be paid three shillings weekly as relief.

There is nothing to interest us until 27 December 1788, when we find this minute:

> "The Brethren having Selebrated the Anniversary of St John in the usual manner and Brother Burns of Aelliesland of St Davids Strabolton Lodge No. 178 being present The Lodge unanimously Assumed him a member of the Lodge being a Master Masson he Subscribed the regulations as a member
> Thereafter the Lodge was Shut.
>
> Sim. Mackenzie"

Brother John Aiken was Master when Burns joined – he was filling the chair for the fourth time – but was absent at this meeting and a Brother Burgess, who had been Deputy for years, but never was Master, presided to receive the new affiliate.

The Minute of April 1790 states that five members convened in the George Tavern – Burns being one of them. In December of this year Burns, who was now living in Dumfries, was present along with his friend and fellow-Gauger, Finlayter, when cards of excuse were read and sustained, "Thereafter the Lodge was shut". Perhaps the fullest minute in Burns' time was the next, dated 6 February 1792.

"At a meeting of Dumfries St Andrews Lodge held this evening Present The Right Worshipful Master (with seven other office bearers five of them acting *p.t.* Burns as a steward). Brother James Hay, Writer to the Signet, a brother of Saint David's Edinburgh, and Bro. Lieut. Wm Millar, second son of the family of Dalswinton a brother of the Thistle Lodge Edinburgh, were visitors, when Mr Philip Ditcher was entered an apprentice. Thereafter the said Brothers Hay and Miller, were assumed Bretheren and Members of this Lodge."

The Brother Millar referred to afterwards became Provincial Grand Master of the Province, and, as such, laid the foundation stone of the Mausoleum at Dumfries.

Burns was present at meetings on 14 and 31 May, 5 June and 22 November 1792. On 30 November 1792 Burns was elected Senior Warden. "Thereafter the Lodge dined together, and after dinner the same was opened and the evening spent in pleasant mirth and cordiality."

The opening of the "dinner" seems to have been too much for St Andrew, for the Brethren did not meet again until the anniversary night, when Burns goes out of office, and Finlayter goes in as Junior Warden. Another year and they celebrate 29 November, no meeting being held in the interval, but Finlayter is promoted to Senior Warden. No meeting at all in 1785, but on 29 January 1796 Burns recommends as a brother, Mr James Georgeson, Merchant in Liverpool, and the minute narrates:

"The Brethren unanimously agree that Bro. Georgeson's fees shall be applied towards defraying the expenses of this night."

Another meeting was held in the Coffee House on 14 April 1796, when "Caledonia's Bard, Brother Burns", made his final appearance on the Masonic Stage. Three months and a few days after, the curtain had finally rung down on the Prologue – Scotland and the World had lost for ever a phenomenal personality, a consummate genius, a master craftsman, but! The Poet lives on, Immortal, and that heritage is ours.

By the generous gift in 1879 of the Grand Master, Sir Michael Shaw Stewart, the Grand Lodge of Scotland now owns (1) The Minute Book of the Lodge St Andrew, No. 179, of which Burns was an affiliated Member, bearing the Poet's signature to the Bye-laws, and containing the Minute of his admission, (2) The Mallet of St Andrew and (3) An Apron used in the Lodge in Burns' time.

Burns' Masonic Rhymes and Allusions to Masonry in his Letters

Chamber's "Life and Works" – Wallace Edition –
"No Churchman am I", Vol. 1, page 130, year 1784.

A Stanza added in a Mason Lodge
> Then fill up a bumper and make it o'erflow,
> And honours masonic prepare for to throw;
> May every true Brother of the Compass and Square
> Having a big-belly'd bottle when harass'd with care.

Epistle to J. Lapraik. Vol. I, page 162, year 1785.
    But ye whom social pleasure charms,
    Whose heart the tide of kindness warms,
    Who hold your being on the terms,
                "Each aid the others",
    Come to my bowl, come to my arms,
                My friends, my brothers!

Second Epistle to Davie. Vol I, page 211, year 1785.
    For me, I'm on Parnassus brink,
    Rivin the words tae gar them clink;
    Whyles daez't wi' love, whyles daez't wi' drink,
                Wi' jads or masons;
    An' whyles, but ay ower late, I think
                Braw sober lessons.

Address to the Deil. Vol. I, page 225, year 1785.
    When masons' mystic word an' grip,
    In storms an' tempests raise you up,
    Some cock or cat your rage maun stop,
                Or, strange to tell!
    The youngest "brither" ye wad whip
                Aff straught to hell.

Letter to David Brice, Glasgow. Vol. I, page 345, year 1786.
"I have tried often to forget her", (*i.e.* Jean Armour), "I have run into all kinds of dissipation and riot, mason-meetings, drinking-matches, and other mischief, to drive her out of my head, but all in vain."

Dedication to Gavin Hamilton, Esq. Vol. I, page 376, year 1786.
    If friendless, how, we meet together,
    Then, sir, your hand, – my Friend and Brother!

The Farewell to the Brethren of Lodge St James, Tarbolton.
Vol. I, page 376, year 1786.
        Adieu! a heart-warm, fond adieu!
        Dear brothers of the *mystic tie*!
        Ye favour'd, ye *enlighten'd* few;
        Companions of my social joy!
        Tho' I to foreign lands must hie,
        Pursuing Fortune's slidd'ry ba',
        With melting heart, and brimful eye,
        I'll mind you still, tho' far away.

        Oft have I met your social Band,
        And spent the chearful, festive night;
        Oft, honor'd with supreme command,
        Presided o'er the *Sons of light:*
        And by that *Hieroglyphic* bright,

125

Which none but *Craftsmen* ever saw!
Strong Mem'ry on my heart shall write
Those happy scenes when far awa!

May Freedom, Harmony and Love,
Unite you in the *grand Design,*
Beneath th' Omniscient Eye above,
The glorious *Architect* Divine!
That you may keep th' *unerring line,*
Still rising by the *plummet's law,*
Till *Order* bright completely shine,
Shall be my pray'r when far awa.

And *You,* farewell! whose merits claim
Justly that *highest badge* to wear!
Heav'n bless your honor'd, noble Name,
, To *Masonry* and *Scotia* dear!
A last request permit me here,
When yearly ye assemble a',
One *round,* I ask it with a *tear,*
To him, *the Bard that's far awa.*

Lines to Dr Mackenzie, Mauchline. Vol I, page 378, year 1786.
Friday first's the day appointed
By the Right Worshipful anointed,
To hold our grand procession;
To get a blad o' Johnie's morals,
And taste a swatch o' Manson's barrels
I' the way of our profession.
The Master and the Brotherhood
Would a' be glad to see you;
For me I would be mair than proud
To share the mercies wi' you
If Death, then, wi' skaith, then,
Some mortal heart is hechtin,
Inform him, and storm him,
That Saturday you'll fecht him.

Ye Sons of Old Killie. Vol. I, page 379, year 1786.
Ye sons of old Killie, assembled by Willie,
To follow the noble vocation;
Your thrifty old mother has scarce such another
To sit in that honoured station.
I've little to say, but only to pray,
As praying's the ton of your fashion;
A prayer from the Muse you well may excuse,
'Tis seldom her favourite passion.

126

Ye powers who preside o'er the wind and the tide,
Who markèd each element's border;
Who formèd this frame with beneficent aim,
Whose sovereign statute is order:–
Within this dear mansion, may wayward Contention
Or withered Envy ne'er enter;
May secrecy round be the mystical bound,
And brotherly Love be the centre!

Tam Samson's Elegy. Vol. 1, page 405, year 1786.
The Brethren o' the mystic "level"
May hing their head in wofu' bevel,
While by their nose the tears will revel,
             Like ony bead;
Death's gien the Lodge an unco devel,
                Tam Samson's dead!

Letter to John Ballantine. Vol. 11, page 37, year 1787.
"I went to a Mason-lodge yesternight when the Most Worshipful Grand Master Charters (Charteris) and all the Grand lodge of Scotland visited. The meeting was most numerous and elegant; all the different Lodges about town were present in all their pomp. The Grand Masters who presided with great solemnity, and honour to himself as a Gentleman and Mason, among other general toasts gave, 'Caledonia, and Caledonia's Bard brother B' – which rung through the whole Assembly with multiplied honors and repeated acclamations. As I had no idea such a thing would happen, I was downright thunderstruck, and trembling in every nerve made the best return in my power. Just as I finished, some of the Grand Officers said so loud as I could hear, with a most comforting accent, 'Very well indeed', which set me something to rights again."

Burns Journal of the Border Tour. Vol. II, page 114, year 1787.
"Saturday (May 19) – Spent the day at Mr Grieve's – made a Royal Arch Mason of St Abb's Lodge. Mr Wm. Grieve, the oldest brother, a joyous, warm-hearted, jolly, clever fellow – takes a hearty glass, and sings a good song. Mr Robert, his brother, and partner in trade, a good fellow, but says little – take a sail after dinner – fishing of all kinds pays tithes at Eyemouth."

Letter to Robert Ainslie. Vol. II, page 128, Year 1787.
"MY DEAR FRIEND AND BROTHER ARCH,"

Letter to James Smith, Linlithgow. Vol. II, page 132, year 1787.
"I have yet fixed on nothing with respect to the serious business of life. I am, just as usual, a rhyming, mason-making, rattling, aimless, idle, fellow. However, I shall somewhere have a farm soon."

Letter to Lodge St James. Vol. II, page 148, year 1787.
"MEN AND BRETHREN – I am truly sorry it is not in my power to be at your quarterly meeting. If I must be absent in body, believe me I shall be present in

spirit. I suppose those who owe us monies, by bill or otherwise, will appear – I mean those we summoned. If you please, I wish you would delay prosecuting defaulters till I come home. The court is up, and I will be home before it sits down. In the meantime, to take a note of those who appear and who do not, of our faulty debtors, will be right in my humble opinion; and those who confess debt and crave days, I think we should spare them. Farewell"

> "Within your dear mansion may wayward Contention
>   And withered Envy ne'er enter;
> May Secrecy round be the mystical bound,
>   And brotherly Love be the centre."

Epistle to Hugh Parker. Vol. II, page 347, year 1788.
> "Tarbolton, twenty-fourth o' June,
> Ye'll find me in a better tune;"

To James Tennant of Glenconner. Vol. III, page 78, year 1789.
> "My auld school fellow, preacher Willie;
> The manly tar, my mason-Billie;"

There is exant a Mason Apron, bearing on the underside of the "flap" this inscription:
> "Charles Sharpe of Holtham, to Rabbie Burns"
>   "Dumfries, Dec. 12, 1791."

A Man's a man for a' that. Vol. IV, page 187, year 1795.
We do not believe Burns ever intended any part of this song to be Masonic. On the other hand, there are some who consider the last verse to "Breath the very spirit of Masonry", and that verse is quoted without prejudice.

> Then let us pray that come it may, –
> As come it will for a' that –
> That Sense and Worth, o'er a' the earth,
> May bear the gree, and a' that.
> For a'' that, and a' that,
> It's comin' yet for a' that,
> That Man to Man, the world o'er
> Shall brothers be for a' that!

EDITOR'S FOOTNOTE TO CHAPTER FIFTEEN
The errors noted are minimal. Readers will, before reaching this section, have been aware of them and their corrections.

The Final Chapter

An Appraisal

THE INFLUENCE OF FREEMASONRY ON ROBERT BURNS

Brother Rev I. U. Macdonald, Lodge 135
Lodge Chaplain, Chaplain Provincial Grand Lodge of Ayrshire:
Worshipful Past Senior Grand Chaplain.

Over the years it has been a wonderful personal experience to hear so many erudite, articulate, speakers propose the toast, "The Immortal Memory of Robert Burns". For the most part each address has been thoroughly researched and each has been a revelation on how diverse are the themes chosen to express the individual speaker's thoughts of what he regards has made Robert Burns "the world acclaimed poet of the centuries". I have sat at the feet of men whose backgrounds span the social, intellectual, religious divides of the world and learned.

It would be a life time's occupation to read and study in depth every book, magazine and paper which has been published on the subject "Robert Burns". Of the books I have read it is interesting to note the wide diversity of opinion, of emphasis, of appreciation authors have employed as to their thoughts on the life and works of Robert Burns.

During my term as Grand Chaplain it was my duty and privilege to be a member of a deputation from the Grand Lodge of Scotland as it conducted the Ceremony of Rededication of a Lodge to mark a milestone in the history of that Lodge. From Orkney in the North to Hawick in the South; from Oban in the West to Montrose in the East I travelled with my Brothers and I cannot remember one lodge which did not have either a portrait or a likeness cast in some material or other of Robert Burns. My mother Lodge is known as Lodge Tarbolton Kilwinning St James, No. 135, The Lodge of Robert Burns and rightly so. Above the Master's Chair there is placed such a likeness so that all the business conducted comes under his watchful eye. Such portraits are not only displayed within Lodges but are to be found in such diverse places as clubs and pubs; in shops and supermarkets, in town halls and city squares the world o'er. This is a visual proclamation of the importance attached to Burns in the ongoing life of craft, commerce and community.

It is obvious that Robert Burns has had an incalculable influence on uncountable millions over these two hundred years. To claim that, through his prose and poetry, he has influenced men and women in almost every country in the world and continues to do so is no exaggeration. Despite all the speeches given, all the chapters written, all the portraits painted and statues or statuettes erected, all in their own way reminding us of the influence Burns has exerted, there is little about what influenced him and in particular what influence, if any, Freemasonry had on his whole life.

Elsewhere the Masonic life of Robert Burns is dealt with. From the day he was initiated into Freemasonry it would seem that he found a purpose and meaning and dignity in life that had so far eluded him. The young Lochlie embraced the Craft and its tenets with enthusiasm and by his keen observations and subtle mind he soon found that he had come where he was given a sense of belonging and fulfilment. Thus began a life-long love of and for Freemasonry and the Brotherhood.

It is no surprise that the eager, keen, bright, young Brother Robert was quickly advanced and as his studious mind explored the allegorical teachings of the Craft he became more and more enamoured by its powerful influence for good over those who embraced and lived by its tenets. For Robert personally his initiation gave him a self-confidence he had never thought possible. Then as now there was a social divide in society. Though that divide has narrowed significantly the 18th Century Scot was burdened by the tradition that one should live, work, marry and die within the social station into which he or she was born. Many found this barrier frustrating and soul destroying. It was difficult to break away from such a tradition but some did and many more tried through hard work or education or astute business ventures and Burns was no different. Like it or not he was the son of a tenant farmer, not a very prosperous one, and as such had the yoke of hard labour and poverty strapped to his person. He was in the eyes of his peer group just a poor tenant farmer's son. Nothing more, nothing less. It hurt and angered the keen and sensitive mind of the poet ploughman to be judged solely on his social status. In his poem, written when only eighteen years of age, "O Tibbie I Have Seen The Day" this hurt and anger is expressed in the line, "Ye geck at me because I'm poor". Tibbie Stein [or Steven] had turned from Robert to a more prosperous suitor simply because of his financial circumstances. This was not to be a "one-off" experience as the Alison Begbie affair was to prove.

He was trapped in an economic and social void before being initiated into Freemasonry. There within the Lodge he found a level playing field which he had never before experienced. Within the Lodge there were no lords or labourers, no farmers or cotters, no rich or poor, all were fellow masons working together within the framework of an honourable craft. It was within the Lodge that Burns came to appreciate a man's worth was not in what he possessed but in what was in his heart.

"The heart aye's the part aye
That makes us right or wrang."
(Epistle to Davie, A Brother Poet)

From this newfound confidence there came among others the amazing poem *The Cotter's Saturday Night* where the reader is given not just a social history of 18th century Scotland, but also a deep insight into the mind of the poet who had the confidence now to recognise and proclaim that the worth of a man is measured not by what he has but by what he is; the worth of a nation lies in the honesty and integrity of its people no matter who or what they are.

Freemasonry gave the young Robert Burns the confidence to be himself. It also gave him a credibility which would have been difficult to obtain in the literary circles of his generation. One cannot, of course, be categorical as to how long it would have taken a ploughman poet from rural Ayrshire to be accepted, if ever, within such cloistered circles. The fact is that he was accepted and accepted as an accredited poet. The key that opened the door to this acceptance came through men who were like himself – Freemasons. In October 1786 Burns was made an honorary member of Lodge St John, 22, Kilmarnock. The minute of the Lodge on that date concludes: "Robert Burns, poet, from Mauchline, a member of St James, Tarbolton, was made an honorary member of the Lodge". It must have given Brother Robert great pleasure to have been referred to as a "poet".

A greater accolade awaited him a few months later while attending a meeting in Lodge Edinburgh St Andrew, 48 at which the Grand Master and his office-bearers were present. Charteris, afterwards Lord Elcho, the Grand Master proposed the toast in the words: "Caledonia and Caledonia's Bard, Robert Burns". This honour came as a complete surprise for in a letter to his friend, Ballantine, he wrote, "As I had no idea such a thing would happen, I was downright thunderstruck and, trembling in every nerve, made the best return in my power".

In that august company were men of distinction, Masons all, who were impressed by the fine oratory and natural charisma of the recipient of the Grand Master's toast for in that same letter to his friend, Burns further wrote, "Just as I had finished, some of the Grand Officers said, so loud that I could hear, with a most comforting accent: 'Very well indeed!' which set me something to rights again." The following month, February 1787, Burns was made a member of Lodge Canongate Kilwinning, 2, introduced by the Hon. Henry Erskine the famous advocate where he would have, no doubt, made the acquaintance of further influential brother masons. Through the many contacts made in Masonic Lodges one was to prove vital to the future life of the Bard. William Creech became the publisher of the Edinburgh edition of his Poems which gave so many more people the opportunity to read his poems. There is one name which cannot be omitted and that is Glencairn. During this first visit to the capital city Robert was introduced to James, Earl of Glencairn and from that first meeting there was forged a life-long friendship. In Robert's heart there always was a very special place for Brother James, Earl of Glencairn. The Earl became his mentor, his adviser, his benefactor and this produced in him a deep sense of gratitude, respect and regard shown by an entry in his diary part of which reads, "Though I should never see him (Glencairn) more, I shall love him to my dying day". Professor Dugald Stewart of Edinburgh University was a man of powerful intellect who met Burns while holidaying in Catrine, Ayrshire. Both men made a profound impression on each other and while Depute Master of St James Tarbolton it was Robert's honour to make Brother Stewart an Honorary member of his Mother Lodge. Through the good offices of his Masonic Brethren Burns entered into the world of professional giants, of high society and of the "literati" of the Capital. There he entered and there he was accepted, pampered and acclaimed. Truly the ploughman poet had become "Caledonia's Bard". The influence that this "Capital-experience" had on Robert Burns cannot be underestimated yet through it all he remained his own man.

James Mackay in his authoritative and informative biography of Robert Burns quotes from a letter written by Dugald Stewart in which the eminent professor writes, "The attention he (Burns) received during his stay in town from all ranks and descriptions of persons, were such as would have turned any head but his own".

I have concentrated on Burns's short stay in Edinburgh during the winter months of 1786/87 to illustrate the influence Freemasonry played in presenting him as a serious poet in whom the Muse found a happy home. What Robert Burns would have achieved without Freemasonry is but idle speculation. What can be asserted is that he was a Freemason and because of that he was influenced by its tenets and by those who expounded them in Lodge and lived by them in life.